LEARN TO
knit

LEARN TO
knit

EDITED BY
Sue Whiting

PHOTOGRAPHS BY
John Heseltine

Sterling Publishing Co., Inc.
New York

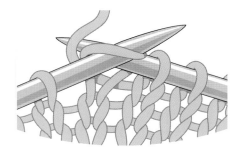

Editor Sally Harding
Design Anne Wilson
Illustrations Kate Simunek
Photography John Heseltine
Styling Susan Berry

Library of Congress Cataloging-in-Publication Data Available

10 9 8 7 6 5 4 3 2 1

Published by Sterling Publishing Co., Inc.
387 Park Avenue South, New York, NY 10016
Copyright © 2005 Coats Crafts UK
Distributed in Canada by Sterling Publishing
c/o Canadian Manda Group, 165 Dufferin
Street, Toronto, Ontario, Canada M6K 3H6

Sterling ISBN 1-4027-2867-0

For information about custom editions, special sales, premium and corporate purchases, please contact Sterling Special Sales Department at 800-805-5489 or specialsales@sterlingpub.com.

Contents

Introduction	6
Techniques	
Needle types and sizes	8
Gauge	9
Casting on	10
Working with four needles	13
Knitting basics	14
Continental knitting	15
Knit stitch	16
Purl stitch	17
Shaping	18
Binding off	20
Finishing touches	21
Gallery of projects	
Pot holder	26
Cushion cover	28
Tea cozy	30
Baby slipover	32
Crib blanket	34
Baby slippers	38
Girl's bolero	40
Child's gloves	44
Child's wool cardigan	46
Child's cotton sweaters	50
Child's raglan sweaters	54
Unisex V-neck sweater	58
Pompom hats	62
Cabled sweater	64
Woman's cotton cardigan	68
Boot socks	72
Wool gloves	75
Knitting abbreviations	78
Index	79
Suppliers and acknowledgments	80

Introduction

When learning to knit, you need to understand how knitting is created and what tools you will need. To make a flat piece of knitting, you work with two needles and a continuous length of yarn, which can be natural fibers, such as wool, cotton, or silk, or manmade ones, such as nylon or acrylic. The finished pieces are then stitched together to make a garment or other project. If you want to make a tubular item, you need to use a circular needle or four double-pointed needles.

The projects in this book are starred in terms of complexity, but none of them is difficult. The introduction to each garment explains those suitable for first-time knitters.

The materials and tools you will need include the yarn and the knitting needles, plus scissors, ruler, and blunt-ended tapestry needle The look of your knitting will be determined to a large extent by the chosen yarn and the types of stitches used. Today, there are many different kinds of yarn available, including all forms of fancy and novelty yarns. In this book, we have chosen standard yarns that knit up well and keep their shape after washing.

Yarns

The character of any yarn is determined by its composition and thickness.

Pure wool This has great insulation: warm in winter and cool in summer. Soft and springy, it is comfortable and absorbent. Treated pure wools are machine washable.

Cotton, linen, and silk These create an attractive finish but have little natural elasticity. As a result, they are often combined with other fibers that have these properties. They are comfortable to wear next to the skin but linen and silk are relatively expensive.

Four basic yarns are used in this book. From left to right: lightweight cotton, lightweight wool, medium-weight wool, and Aran-weight wool.

Acrylic A manmade fiber, it is lighter than wool and cheaper. It can be machine washed and dries quickly, but lacks the natural springiness and flexibility of wool.

Nylon Also manmade, this fiber also lacks the springiness of wool but is relatively inexpensive.

Blended fibers Most yarn manufacturers now blend different fibers to produce attractive yarns with textural effects, known as novelty yarns.

Yarn weights The most common generic yarn weights are: fine fingering yarn, often used for baby wear; sport yarn, a lightweight yarn; knitting worsted, a medium-weight yarn; and Aran yarn, a bulky-weight yarn. Extra-bulky yarns are also available for working on giant knitting needles.

Needle types and sizes

Knitting needles come in a range of sizes, from very fine to really fat (see list opposite). A range of materials are used for them, including steel, plastic, and, most recently, bamboo (as shown below). It is important to choose needles that feel comfortable in your hands, and that allow the stitches to slide along easily.

The type of yarn and style of pattern will determine the needle size you use.

Generally, most garments require an average-size needle. The edges on a garment are often knitted in a rib stitch on a size smaller needle than the main body, as this gives the ribbing extra elasticity.

If you are knitting seamless garments, you will need to use a circular needle (see below center) or four needles (see page 13). Garments with more stitches than usual may require a long circular needle.

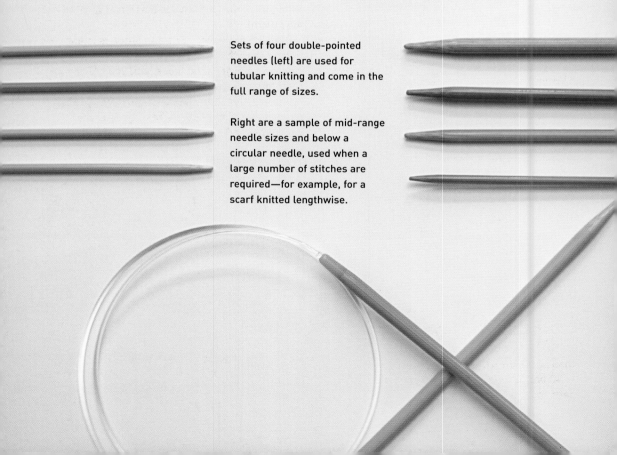

Sets of four double-pointed needles (left) are used for tubular knitting and come in the full range of sizes.

Right are a sample of mid-range needle sizes and below a circular needle, used when a large number of stitches are required—for example, for a scarf knitted lengthwise.

Gauge

Comparative needle sizes

EU METRIC	OLD UK	UK METRIC	US
2mm	14	2mm	0
	13	2¼mm	1
2½mm			
	12	2¾mm	2
3mm	11	3mm	
	10	3¼mm	3
3½mm	9	3¾mm	5
4mm	8	4mm	6
4½mm	7	4½mm	7
5mm	6	5mm	8
5½mm	5	5½mm	9
6mm	4	6mm	10
6½mm	3	6½mm	10½
7mm	2	7mm	
7½mm	1	7½mm	
8mm	0	8mm	11
9mm	00	9mm	13
10mm	000	10mm	15

To make a successful hand-knitted garment to the chosen size, it is essential that you work to the stated gauge—the correct number of stitches and rows over a 4in (10cm) square. To check that your own gauge is the same as that of the pattern, you need to make a small sample square approximately 5in (12cm) in size BEFORE you start to knit a pattern. You then smooth out the sample square, taking care not to stretch the fabric, and count the stitches and rows to 4in (10cm).

If there are fewer rows and stitches to 4in (10cm) than those specified in your pattern, your own gauge is too loose, and you therefore need to use a size smaller needle. If you have too many stitches and rows, your gauge is too tight, and a size larger needle will be needed.

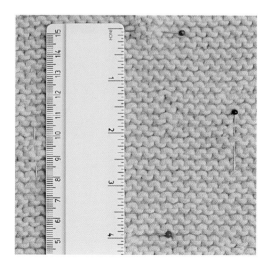

Notes for patterns

The patterns in this book are graded as easy (✪), intermediate (✪✪), and advanced (✪✪✪). Novice knitters should start with those marked ✪.

Abbreviations generally used in all patterns are given on page 78.

Casting on

To make the very first loops on your needles, you "cast on" stitches. There are several methods, but all of them require you, in the first place, to create an initial loop on your needle. A commonly used technique is shown here. All cast-on loops should be made as evenly as possible. Avoid casting on too tightly. The cast-on stitches should slide freely on the needle.

Making the first loop

1 Wrap the yarn around the first and second fingers of one hand as shown.

2 Place the tip of the needle under the first loop as shown, catch the other loop with the needle and draw it through.

3 Withdraw your fingers from the loop, then tighten it on the needle to form the first stitch.

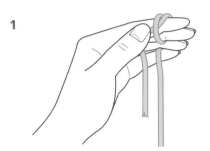

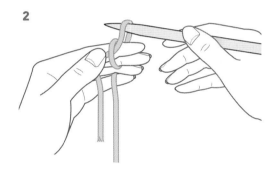

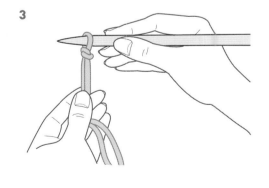

Thumb cast-on

This is a common, and easy, method of casting on. The tail end of the yarn is held in the right hand and the ball end of the yarn (also called the working yarn) is held in the left hand.

1 With the initial loop on the needle, held in the right hand, hold the working yarn in the palm of the left hand, as shown, passing it around the thumb. If necessary to keep the loop on the needle in place, hold the tail end of the yarn with the right hand. Pass the tip of the needle from front to back under the front strand of yarn on the thumb as shown by the arrow.

2 With the strand of yarn around your thumb caught by the needle, gently slip your left thumb out of the loop.

3 Tighten the new loop on the needle, but make sure it will still glide along the needle. You have now made the second cast-on loop.

4 Reinsert your left thumb under the working yarn to begin the next cast-on loop. Continue to cast on stiches by repeating steps 1 through 3.

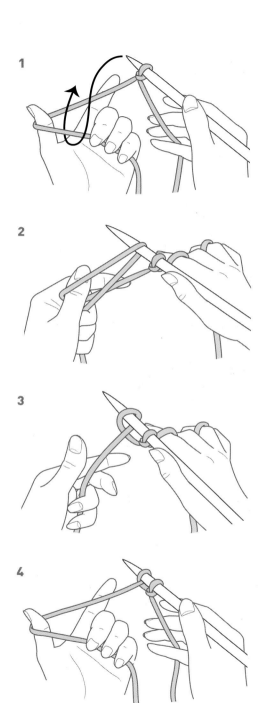

1

2

3

4

Chain-edge cast-on

This cast-on method gives a looser edge than the thumb cast-on, although it can be tightened to create a firmer, more elastic edge by knitting into the back of the stitches on the next row. (If you are a complete beginner, turn to pages 14 and 15 before you try this cast-on to find out how to hold the needles and yarn.)

1 Make a starting loop on the needle as already described (see page 10) and hold this needle in your left hand. Hold the ball end of the yarn and the other needle in your right hand. Insert the right needle through the loop as shown and pass the yarn around the tip.

2 With the tip of the right needle, pull the yarn through the loop on the left needle to create a new loop on the right needle.

3 Transfer this new loop onto the left needle, by inserting the tip of the left needle from right to left through the front of the loop. Withdraw the right needle, then reinsert it through the loop just made, as shown, to start the next cast-on stitch. Repeat steps 1 through 3 to cast on as many stitches as you need.

1
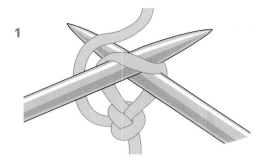

2
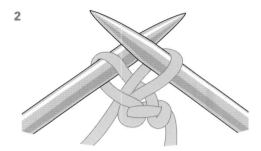

3
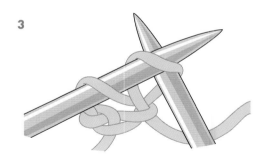

Working with four needles

When you want to knit a tube, without a seam, you use four needles rather than two. When you knit, you simply work clockwise around three needles, using the fourth as the working needle. First, of course, you have to cast on stitches onto three of the four needles. A chain-edge cast-on is recommended.

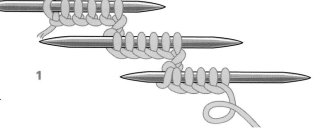

1

Cast on with four needles

1 Using the chain-edge cast-on, cast on the stitches onto one needle, then divide them evenly between the three needles.

2 To start to knit, arrange the three needles in a triangle. The working yarn will be at the end of the third needle.

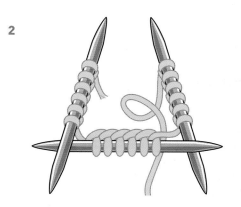

2

3 Place a colored thread or a stitch marker on the needle next to the working yarn to mark the start of the rounds. Then start to knit with the fourth needle, closing the cast-on triangle when knitting through the first stitch on the first needle.

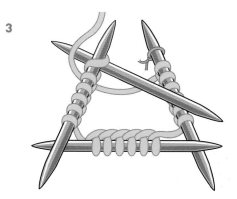

3

Knitting basics

There are only two basic stitches in knitting: knit and purl. All knitted fabrics are made using combinations, or variations, of these stitches.

   To begin, you need to learn how to hold your needles and yarn. Most garments are knitted with two needles (see page 13 to create tubular knitting with four needles). If you are right handed, hold the needle with the existing stitches in your left hand and the working needle and yarn in your right hand. Most people thread the yarn through the right hand, with the ball end of the yarn

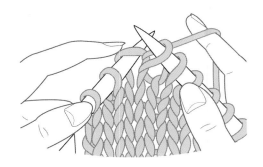

around the little finger, under the third and fourth fingers, and over the index finger, which controls the movement of the yarn.

Continental knitting

A different method of holding the yarn, known as Continental knitting, is preferred by some. With practice, it can make knitting quicker. In it, the left hand controls the yarn and the right hand controls the needle. The hands are held over the top of the work, and the left needle is held between the thumb and second finger, leaving the left hand index finger free to work the yarn, which is looped around the finger.

How to work the knit stitch
1 Keeping the yarn at the back of the work, insert the tip of the right needle into the front of the first stitch on the left needle. Grab the working yarn with the tip of the right needle and pull it through to the front.

2 Allow the stitch on the left needle to slip off, leaving a new stitch on the right needle. Continue in this way to the end of the row. Then turn to start the next row.

How to work the purl stitch
3 Keeping the working yarn at the front of the work, insert the right needle from right to left through the front of the first stitch on the left needle.

4 Take the yarn over and around the needle, then pull it through to the back of the work, controlling the work as shown. Slip the old stitch off the left needle, leaving a new stitch on the right needle. Continue in this way.

1

2

3

4
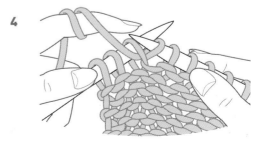

Knit stitch

This is the first stitch you learn and is abbreviated in knitting patterns as k. It creates a simple ridged fabric known as garter stitch when worked on its own. When worked in alternate rows with purl stitch (opposite), it forms a smooth textured stitch known as stockinette stitch (right). Knit

Stockinette stitch is created by alternating knit and purl rows. The knit side is the right side.

stitches are formed by inserting the tip of the knitting needle through from front to back of each stitch, passing the yarn around the needle and drawing a loop through.

How to work the knit stitch

1 Insert the tip of the right needle through the first loop on the left needle, from front to back. Then wrap the working yarn around the tip of the right needle.

2 Pull the tip of the right needle and the yarn through the loop on the left needle.

3 Slip the old loop off the left needle to complete the stitch. Continue knitting stitches in this way until all the stitches on the left needle have been knitted onto the right needle. You have now completed one row of the knit stitch.

1

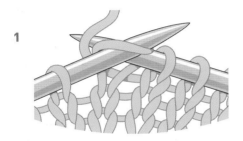

2

3

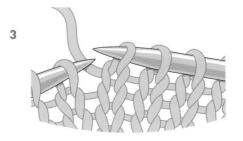

Purl stitch

This is the second stitch to learn and is very similar to the knit stitch. If all rows are purled a garter stitch fabric is created. When purl rows are combined alternately with knit rows, they form stockinette stitch. The purl side of the stockinette stitch fabric is called reverse stockinette stitch. When a purl stitch

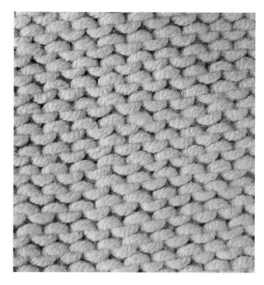

On reverse stockinette stitch, the right side of the fabric is the purl side.

1

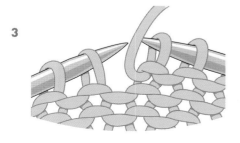

2

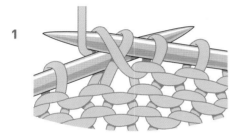

3

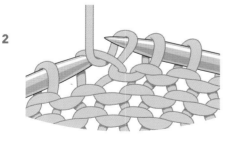

is worked the yarn is held at the front of the work rather than at the back of the work as with the knit stitch.

How to work the purl stitch

1 Insert the right needle through the front of the first stitch on the left needle from right to left and wrap the working yarn around the tip of the needle as shown.

2 With the tip of the right needle, pull the yarn through the loop on the left needle.

3 Slip the old loop off the left needle, leaving a new stitch on the right needle. This completes the purl stitch. Continue in the same way until all the stitches on the left needle have been purled. This completes one purl row.

Shaping

You shape your knitting by adding or subtracting stitches from the rows, as you work. There are various methods of adding and subtracting stitches to create different styles and effects.

Increasing

The first two increasing techniques given below are usually used near the edges of the knitting for side shaping. All the increases are shown worked on a knit row, but the same simple principles can be used with purl stitches (see page 17).

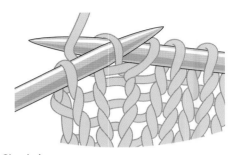

Simple increase

SIMPLE INCREASE

Knit into the front of the stitch in the usual way. But before slipping the old stitch off the needle, knit into the back of the stitch, forming two stitches on the right needle.

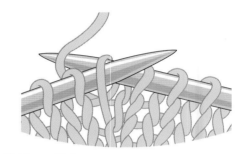

Making a stitch

MAKING A STITCH

This method is different from a simple increase in that it does not use an existing stitch to make another stitch. It is abbreviated as M1 in patterns. Pick up the horizontal loop between two stitches and work into the back of it to make a stitch, as shown. To make two stitches, referred to as M2 in patterns, work into the front of the loop after first working into the back of it.

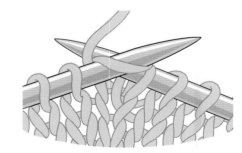

Invisible increase

INVISIBLE INCREASE

This is ideal for increasing in the middle of a row as it is virtually invisible. Knit into the stitch below the next stitch on the left needle, then knit the stitch above as usual.

Decreasing

Decreases are made by working two stitches as one. The joined loops of knitting slope either to the right or left depending on the technique used. If used for decorative purposes, decreases are carefully chosen to create the right detail.

SIMPLE KNIT DECREASE (RIGHT)

This forms a decrease that slopes to the right. Knit two stitches together by inserting the tip of the right needle through the next two stitches instead of one, and knitting these together as one stitch. This is called k2tog.

SIMPLE KNIT DECREASE (LEFT)

This forms a decrease that slopes to the left. Knit two stitches together but insert the tip of the right needle through the back of the stitches. This is called k2tog tbl.

ALTERNATIVE KNIT DECREASE (LEFT)

This also forms a decrease that slopes to the left. Slip one stitch knitwise onto the right needle without knitting it, knit the next stitch, then pass the slipped stitch over the knit stitch and off the right needle.

SIMPLE PURL DECREASE (RIGHT)

This forms a right slope on the knit side of the fabric. Insert the needle purlwise through two stitches and purl them together as one stitch—called p2tog.

Although the knit decreases shown above can be adapted to create purl decreases (by simply purling instead of knitting the stitches) both increases and decreases are usually worked on the knit rows where possible, except for intricate stitch textures or knitted lace.

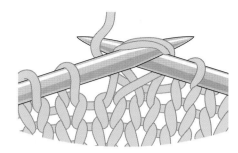

Simple knit decrease (sloping right)

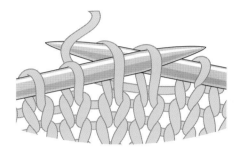

Simple knit decrease (sloping left)

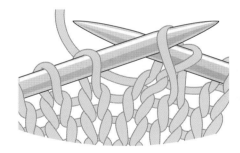

Alternative knit decrease (sloping left)

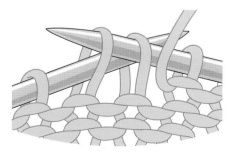

Simple purl decrease (sloping right)

Binding off

The finished bound-off edge.

Once you have completed your knitting, you will need to finish off the work. This is known as binding off. The stitches can be bound off as they are knitted, purled, or worked in a pattern stitch, but the method is the same. The simple knit bind-off is shown below.

1

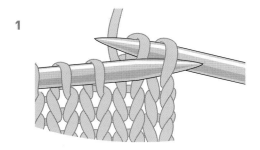

2

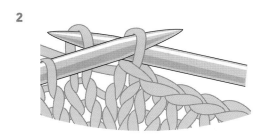

3

How to bind off
Be careful when binding off not to do so too tightly. You can use a size larger needle to avoid this, if you wish.

1 Knit the first two stitches. Then pick up the first stitch with the tip of the left needle and pass it over the second stitch and off the right needle all together, to leave one stitch on the right handle.

2 Now knit the next stitch so there are two stitches again on the right needle. Bind off another stitch by repeating step 1.

3 Continue to bind off stitch by stitch across the row until only one stitch remains. Break the yarn, draw the end through the last stitch, and slip the stitch off the needle. Pull the yarn to fasten off. The tail end will be darned in later when finishing.

Finishing touches

There are a number of useful tips and techniques that will help ensure a professional finish on your garment.

Blocking

When you have finished the various parts of the garment, they should be pressed. Check the yarn label for any pressing instructions. Pin out each piece of knitted fabric, wrong side uppermost, on an ironing sheet and check the measurements against the pattern instructions. Then block out each piece by pinning around the edges, to the size required. Lightly press in place, with a clean, damp cloth between the iron and the knitting. Avoid pressing the ribbing as this lessens its elasticity.

Seams

The majority of garments are made up with a backstitch seam, which gives a tailored finish. For baby garments and delicate fabrics, use a flat seam. For ribbing, use invisible seams.

BACKSTITCH SEAM

Place the two pieces of fabric right sides together, and pin in position. Sew together with a row of backstitches, worked one stitch in from the edge, as shown.

FLAT SEAM

Place the two pieces of fabric right sides together, and pin in position. Sew together with loose overcasting stitches, matching ridge to ridge.

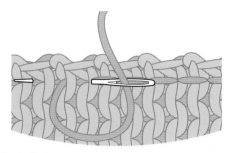

Backstitch seam

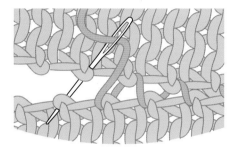

Flat seam

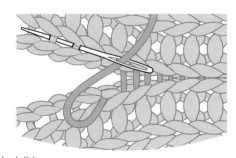

Invisible seam

INVISIBLE SEAM

With the right sides of the knitting facing you, place the two pieces of fabric side by side. Stitch together as shown, working one stitch from each edge in turn, as shown.

Buttonholes and buttonbands

If your garment has separately worked button and buttonhole bands, you should first pin the fronts to the back at shoulder seams. Then pin the bands to the front, taking care to ensure that the lower edge of the garment forms a straight edge. One stitch should be taken from the band and the cardigan to form the seam.

REINFORCED CARDIGAN BANDS

You can create a really professional finish on a cardigan by reinforcing the front bands with grosgrain-ribbon facings. First, pin a facing in place on the wrong side of each band, taking care not to stretch the knitting. Slipstitch the facings in place, as shown. On the buttonhole band, cut the buttonholes in the facing to match the buttonholes on the garment and work buttonhole stitch around each one using a matching sewing thread. Sew the buttons to the button band in corresponding positions.

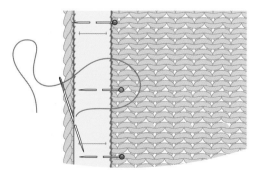

Positioning buttonband facing

BUTTONHOLES

To knit a horizontal buttonhole, work to the position of the buttonhole, bind off one, two, or three stitches, then work to the end of the row. On the next row, cast on the same number of stitches over those bound-off. On the following row, pick up the loose thread at the base of the buttonhole, work the next stitch and pass the picked up stitch over it.

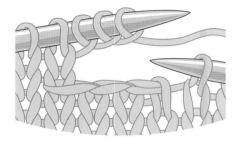

Horizontal buttonhole

To make a vertical buttonhole, divide the stitches at the buttonhole position and work an equal number of rows on each set of stitches, then join up with a row of stitches worked right across.

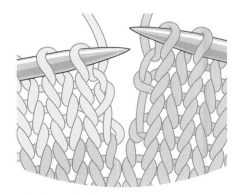

Vertical buttonhole

Neckbands

When you work the neck trimming on a garment, you will usually have to pick up stitches along the edge of the knitting. The following tips help to create a tidy edging.

On a V-neck sweater, a neat appearance is achieved by keeping a single knit stitch up the center front, on the right side of the work. To do this, pick up an even number of stitches on each side of the V and one at the center front, so when you work in k1, p1 rib, this center stitch will always be a k1. The V is shaped by working a decrease on each side of the center k1.

It is easiest to pick up stitches evenly if you divide the edge with pins. If you have 60 stitches to pick up, for example, along the front slope off a cardigan, you can divide this into 10 equal sections with pins and pick up six stitches in each section.

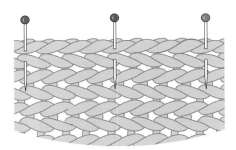

Dividing the neck evenly

Picking up and knitting stitches

When you pick up and knit along bound-off stitches across the front and back of the neck, knit through both loops. This will avoid loose stitches and holes.

A shaped edge where decreases have been worked has an alternate long and short stitch. Knit through all loops as required, spacing them evenly, but work twice into long loops for more stitches or omit some of the long loops for less. When picking up and knitting stitches along the straight side of the neck (through rows), insert the needle through both loops.

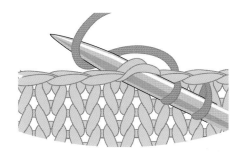

Picking up stitches along bound-off stitches

Picking up dropped stitches

If a stitch is accidentally dropped, it is easiest to use a crochet hook to pick it up, even if it has unraveled a few rows down. To pick up knit stitches, insert the hook into the dropped stitch, catch the bar lying above the dropped stitch and pull it through. To pick up purl stitches, simply turn the work over and use the same method as for knit stitches.

Joining in new yarn

Whenever possible, join a new ball of yarn at the beginning of a row. Where a new ball of yarn has to be joined in the middle of a row, you can make a neat join by splicing the yarn. Unravel a short length of the yarn from the old ball and the new one, and cut away a strand or two from each. Twist the remaining strands together to make one thickness of yarn. Knit carefully through this join, trimming off any stray ends.

gallery of projects

Pot holder

⭐ *This little pot holder is worked in three colors, and forms a pocket to insert your hand. The colorwork pattern is created by slipping stitches and using only one color in each row. Slip-stitch colorwork patterns form a dense fabric that is perfect for pot holders.*

You will need

- A wool-mix, medium-weight yarn, each ball approx 1¾oz/131yd (50g/120m):
    1 ball in **MC**—dark blue
    Small amount in each of **A**—light olive green; and **B**—denim blue
- Pair of size 3 (3¼mm) knitting needles
- ¾in (2cm) diameter curtain ring

Gauge and finished size

- 22 stitches and 38 rows to 4in (10cm) over pattern using size 3 (3¼mm) needles.
- Pot holder measures 8in (20.5cm) square.

Front and back (both alike)

With size 3 (3¼mm) needles and MC, cast on 43 sts.
Starting with a k row, work in St st for 2 rows, ending with RS facing for next row.
Join in A and **patt** as foll:
Row 1 (RS) Using A, k1, *sl 1 purlwise, k3; rep from * to last 2 sts, sl 1 purlwise, k1.
Row 2 Using A, k1, bring yarn to front (WS) of work, *sl 1 purlwise, p3; rep from * to last 2 sts, sl 1 purlwise, k1.
Join in B.
Row 3 Using B, k3, *sl 1 purlwise, k3; rep from * to end.
Row 4 Using B, k1, p2, *sl 1 purlwise, p3; rep

from * to last 4 sts, sl 1 purlwise, p2, k1.
Rows 5 and 6 As rows 1 and 2 but using MC.
Rows 7 and 8 As rows 3 and 4 but using A.
Rows 9 and 10 As rows 1 and 2 but using B.
Rows 11 and 12 As rows 3 and 4 but using MC.
These 12 rows form patt.
Rep rows 1 to 12 four times more.
Break off A and B and cont using MC only.

SHAPE END BORDER
Place marker at beg of last row.
Next row (RS) *K2, k2tog tbl; rep from * to last 3 sts, k3. (33 sts)
Work in garter st for 5 rows, inc 1 st at each end of next and foll 2 alt rows. (39 sts) Bind off.

Side border

With RS facing, size 3 (3¼mm) needles, and MC, **pick up and k** 31 sts down row-end edge of front piece, from marker to cast-on edge. Work in garter st for 5 rows, inc 1 st at each end of next and foll 2 alt rows. (37 sts) Bind off. Work one side border on back piece in same way. (Each piece has borders along two sides.)

Finishing

Press following instructions on yarn label. Lay pieces WS facing so that there is a border all around holder and join shaped row-end edges of Borders. Neatly slip stitch cast-on and row-end edges in place, leaving one cast-on edge open.
Using MC, work buttonhole st over curtain ring and attach to a top corner.

Cushion cover

⭐ *This elegant black, white, and gray rectangular cushion looks good in both traditional and contemporary settings. Combine it with other monochrome cushions for a cool urban look, or put it with bright, strong plain colors so that it creates a focal point on a sofa or bed. The slip-stitch colorwork is easy to knit because only one color is used in a row.*

You will need
- A wool-mix, medium-weight yarn, each ball approx 1³/₄oz/131yd (50g/120m):
    3 balls in **MC**—black
    2 balls in each of **A**—gray; and **B**—cream
- Pair each of size 5 (3³/₄mm) and size 6 (4mm) knitting needles
- 14in x 19in (36cm x 48cm) pillow form

Gauge and finished size
- 22 stitches and 30 rows to 4in (10cm) over St st using size 6 (4mm) needles.
- Completed cushion cover measures 14in x 19in (36cm x 48cm).

Special abbreviations
sL2 = slip next 2 sts purlwise.
wyib = with yarn in back (WS) of work.
wyif = with yarn in front (WS) of work.

Front and back (both alike)
With size 5 (3³/₄mm) needles and MC, cast on 76 sts.
Work in garter st for 2 rows, ending with RS facing for next row.
Joining in and breaking off colors as required, **patt** as foll:

Change to size 6 (4mm) needles.
Row 1 (RS) Using A, *k4, sL2 wyib; rep from * to last 4 sts, k4.
Row 2 Using A, *p4, sL2 wyif; rep from * to last 4 sts, p4.
Rows 3 and 4 As rows 1 and 2.
Rows 5 and 6 Using MC, knit.
Join in B.
Row 7 Using B, k1, *sL2 wyib, k4; rep from * to last 3 sts, sL2 wyib, k1.
Row 8 Using B, p1, *sL2 wyif, p4; rep from * to last 3 sts, sL2 wyif, p1.
Rows 9 and 10 As rows 7 and 8.
Rows 11 and 12 Using MC, knit.
Rows 13 to 24 As rows 1 to 12.
Rows 25 to 28 As rows 1 to 4.
Change to size 5 (3³/₄mm) needles.
Rows 29 to 48 Using MC, knit.
These 48 rows form patt.
Rep rows 1 to 48 twice more, then rows 1 to 28 once more, ending with RS facing for next row.
Bind off.

Finishing
Press following instructions on yarn label. With RS facing, join front and back along three sides. Turn RS out. Insert pillow form, then stitch opening closed.

Tea cozy

⭐⭐ *The choice of colors for this retro-style tea cozy will give it its appeal. You can opt for interesting combinations, such as the lavender and lime chosen here.*

You will need
- A wool-mix, medium-weight yarn, each ball approx 1³/₄oz/131yd (50g/120m):
    - 1 ball in **MC**—lavender
    - 1 ball in **CC**—lime green
- Pair of size 7 (4¹/₂mm) knitting needles

Gauge and finished size
- Based on a St st gauge of 21 stitches and 28 rows to 4in (10cm) using size 7 (4¹/₂mm) needles.
- Tea cozy will fit a standard-size teapot.

Special note
The pleats of the tea cozy are formed by the yarn not in use being stranded quite tightly across WS of work. When working WS rows, remember to take the yarn to the front (WS) of the work before changing colors. Twist yarns together at the back of the work where necessary to prevent holes from forming.

First side
With size 7 (4¹/₂mm) needles and MC, cast on 56 sts. Work in garter st for 4 rows, ending with RS facing for next row.
**Join in CC.
Patt as foll:
Row 1 (RS) Using MC k1, *using CC k6, using MC k6; rep from * to last 7 sts, using CC k6, using MC k1.

Rows 2 to 6 As row 1.
Rows 7 to 12 Using MC k7, *using CC k6, using MC k6; rep from * to last st, using MC k1.
Row 13 and 14 As row 1.
Last 2 rows form patt for rest of piece.
Cont in patt for 26 rows more, ending with RS facing for next row.
SHAPE TOP
Beg shaping top as foll:
Row 1 (RS) Using MC k1, *using CC k2tog, k2, k2tog, using MC k2tog, k2, k2tog; rep from * to last 7 sts, using CC k2tog, k2, k2tog, using MC k1. (38 sts)
Row 2 Using MC k1, *using CC k4, using MC k4; rep from * to last 5 sts, using CC k4, using MC k1.
Row 3 Using MC k1, *using CC (k2tog) twice, using MC (k2tog) twice; rep from * to last 5 sts, using CC (k2tog) twice, using MC k1. (20 sts)
Row 4 Using MC k1, *using CC k2, using MC k2; rep from * to last 3 sts, using CC k2, using MC k1.
Row 5 Using MC k1, *using CC k2tog, using MC k2tog; rep from * to last 3 sts, using CC k2tog, using MC k1. (11 sts)
Row 6 Using MC k1, *using CC k1, using MC k1; rep from * to end.**
Break off CC and cont using MC **only**.
Row 7 K1, * M1 (by picking up horizontal loop lying before next st and knitting into back of it), k into front and back of next st to inc 1; rep from * to last st, M1, k1. (30 sts)
Break yarn and leave these 30 sts on a holder.

Second side

With size 7 (4½mm) needles and MC, cast on 56 sts.

Work in garter st for 4 rows, ending with RS facing for next row.

Cont as for First Side from ** to **, using CC in place of MC and MC in place of CC.

Break off CC and cont using MC **only**.

Row 7 K1, * M1, k into front and back of next st to inc 1; rep from * to last st, M1, k1. (30 sts)

Do NOT break yarn but leave these 30 sts on a holder.

Finishing

Do NOT press.

TOP FRILL

With **WS** facing, size 7 (4½mm) needles and MC, k30 from second side, then 30 from first side. (60 sts)

Work in garter st for 9 rows, ending with **WS** facing for next row. Bind off.

Join Sides along row-end edges, leaving openings for handle and spout.

Using two strands each of MC and CC, make a twisted cord approx 12in (30cm) long and knot ends, forming tiny tassels. Thread cord through last two-color row of Sides, pull up tight, and tie in a bow.

The colors are carried across the back of the work, and pulled tight enough to form "pleats" on the front. For other stranded colorwork, take care NOT to pull the yarns so tight!

Baby slipover

✪✪ *This little slipover is just right for a gift for a newborn baby. Make it and the bootees (see page 38), if you wish, as a matching set. As there is no cable needle involved, working the simple cable is easier than it looks—two stitches are simply twisted around each other on every sixth row of the pattern.*

You will need

- 1 [**1**] x 3½oz/230yd (100g/210m) ball of a lightweight cotton yarn in pink
- Pair each of size 2 (2¾mm) and size 3 (3¼mm) knitting needles

Gauge and finished size

- 35 stitches and 36 rows to 4in (10cm) over pattern using size 3 (3¼mm) needles.
- To fit a newborn [**0–3 months**] baby, chest 14 [**16**]in (36 [**41**]cm).
- Knitted chest measurement—15 [**16½**]in (38 [**42**]cm).
- Finished length—8 [**9**]in (20 [**23**]cm)

Back

With size 2 (2¾mm) needles, cast on 59 [**65**] sts.
Rib row 1 (RS) K1, *p1, k1; rep from * to end.
Rib row 2 P1, *k1, p1; rep from * to end.
These 2 rows form rib.
Cont in rib for ¾in (2cm), ending with **WS** facing for next row.
To prepare for twisted-stitch cable patt, inc sts on next row as foll:
Next row (WS) Rib 2 [**4**], *M1 (by picking up horizontal loop lying before next st and knitting into back of it), rib 9 [**8**]; rep from *

to last 3 [**5**] sts, M1, rib 3 [**5**] (66 [**73**] sts).
Change to size 3 (3¼mm) needles and patt as foll:
Row 1 (RS) P2 [**3**], *k2, p3; rep from * to last 4 [**5**] sts, k2, p2 [**3**].
Row 2 K2 [**3**], *p2, k3; rep from * to last 4 [**5**] sts, p2, k2 [**3**].
Rows 3 and 4 As rows 1 and 2.
Row 5 P2 [**3**], *k into front of second st on left needle, then k into front of first st and slip both sts off needle tog, p3; rep from * to last 4 [**5**] sts, k into front of second st on left needle, then k into front of first st and slip both sts off needle tog, p2 [**3**].
Row 6 As row 2.
These 6 rows form patt.
Cont in patt until Back measures 4 [**4½**]in (10 [**11**]cm), ending with RS facing for next row.
SHAPE ARMHOLES
Keeping patt correct, bind off 2 sts at beg of next 2 rows. (62 [**69**] sts)
Dec 1 st at each end of next 5 rows, then on foll 2 [**3**] alt rows (48 [**53**] sts).**
Cont without shaping until armhole meas 4 [**4½**]in (10 [**12**]cm), ending with RS facing for next row.
SHAPE SHOULDERS
Bind off 3 [**4**] sts at beg of next 4 rows, then 4 [**3**] sts at beg of foll 2 rows.
Leave rem 28 [**31**] sts on a holder.

Front

Work as for Back to **.
Work 1 row, ending with RS facing for next row.

SHAPE NECK

Next row (RS) Patt 16 [**17**] sts, work 2 tog, turn and work this side first.

Keeping patt correct, dec 1 st at neck edge on next 7 rows, ending with RS facing for next row. (10 [**11**] sts)

Cont without shaping until Front matches Back to start of shoulder shaping, ending with RS facing for next row.

SHAPE SHOULDER

Bind off 3 [**4**] sts at beg of next and foll alt row. Work 1 row.

Bind off rem 4 [**3**] sts.

With RS facing, slip center 12 [**15**] sts onto a holder, rejoin yarn to rem sts, work 2 tog, patt to end. (17 [**18**] sts)

Complete to match first side, reversing shaping and working an extra row before start of shoulder shaping.

Finishing

Press following instructions on yarn label. Join right shoulder seam.

Neck border

With RS facing and size 2 (2³/4mm) needles, **pick up and k** 27 [**34**] sts down left side of neck, k12 [**15**] from front, **pick up and k** 27 [**34**] sts up right side of neck, then k28 [**31**] from back dec 1 st at center. (93 [**113**] sts)

Starting with rib row 2, work in rib as for Back for 5 rows, ending with RS facing for next row.

Bind off in rib.

Join left shoulder and Neck Border seam.

Armhole borders (both alike)

With RS facing and size 2 (2³/4mm) needles, **pick up and k** 67 [**73**] sts all around armhole edge.

Starting with rib row 2, work in rib as for Back for 5 rows, ending with RS facing for next row.

Bind off in rib.

Join side and Armhole Border seams.

Crib blanket

✪✪ *This leaf-motif crib blanket is fun to work, and will suit more experienced knitters who want to try their hand at an interesting pattern. You make the motifs first, then join them.*

You will need
- 7 x 1³/₄oz/131yd (50g/120m) balls of a wool-mix, medium-weight yarn in green
- Pair each of size 3 (3¹/₄mm) and size 6 (4mm) knitting needles

Gauge and finished size
- One motif measures 3in (8cm) square using size 6 (4mm) needles.
- Blanket measures 21¹/₂in x 27¹/₂in (54cm x 70cm).

Motif (make 48)
With size 6 (4mm) needles, cast on 3 sts.
Row 1 (RS) K3.
Row 2 K1, p1, k1.
Row 3 Inc in first st, k1, inc in last st. (5 sts)
Row 4 Inc in first st, k1, p1, k1, inc in last st. (7 sts)
Row 5 Inc in first st, p1, k3, p1, inc in last st. (9 sts)
Row 6 K3, p3, k3.
Row 7 K2, p1, (k1, yo) twice, k1, p1, k2. (11 sts)
Row 8 K3, p5, k3.
Row 9 K2, p1, k2, yo, k1, yo, k2, p1, k2. (13 sts)
Row 10 K2, inc in next st, p7, inc in next st, k2. (15 sts)
Row 11 K2, p2, k3, yo, k1, yo, k3, p2, k2. (17 sts)

Row 12 K4, p9, k4.
Row 13 K2, p2, k4, yo, k1, yo, k4, p2, k2. (19 sts)
Row 14 K3, inc in next st, p11, inc in next st, k3. (21 sts)
Row 15 K2, p3, k5, yo, k1, yo, k5, p3, k2. (23 sts)
Row 16 K5, p13, k5.
Row 17 K2, p3, k6, yo, k1, yo, k6, p3, k2. (25 sts)
Row 18 K4, inc in next st, p15, inc in next st, k4. (27 sts)
Row 19 K1, inc in next st, p4, k7, yo, k1, yo, k7, p4, inc in next st, k1. (31 sts)
Row 20 K7, p17, k7.
Row 21 K1, k2tog, p4, k7, sL1K, k2tog, psso, k7, p4, k2tog, k1. (27 sts)
Row 22 K4, k2tog, p15, k2tog, k4. (25 sts)
Row 23 K2, p3, k6, sL1K, k2tog, psso, k6, p3, k2. (23 sts)
Row 24 As row 16.
Row 25 K2, p3, k5, sL1K, k2tog, psso, k5, p3, k2. (21 sts)
Row 26 K3, k2tog, p11, k2tog, k3. (19 sts)
Row 27 K2, p2, k4, sL1K, k2tog, psso, k4, p2, k2. (17 sts)
Row 28 As row 12.
Row 29 K2, p2, k3, sL1K, k2tog, psso, k3, p2, k2. (15 sts)
Row 30 K2, k2tog, p7, k2tog, k2. (13 sts)
Row 31 K2, p1, k2, sL1K, k2tog, psso, k2, p1, k2. (11 sts)
Row 32 As row 8.
Row 33 K2, p1, k1, sL1K, k2tog, psso, k1, p1, k2. (9 sts)
Row 34 As row 6.

Row 35 K2, p1, sL1K, k2tog, psso, p1, k2.
(7 sts)
Row 36 K1, k2tog, p1, k2tog, k1. (5 sts)
Row 37 K2tog, k1, k2tog. (3 sts)
Row 38 K3tog and fasten off.

Finishing

Press following instructions on yarn label, pressing each Motif to 8cm (3in) square. Stitch four Motifs tog to form a square with "leaf stems" at center. Join 11 more sets of four Motifs in this way. Then join squares to form a rectangle six Motifs wide and eight Motifs long.

Border

With size 3 (3¼mm) needles, cast on 7 sts.
Row 1 (RS) K7.
Row 2 K3, p1, k3.
Row 3 K2, p1, inc twice in next st, p1, k2.
(9 sts)
Row 4 K3, p3, k3.
Row 5 K2, p1, (k1, yo) twice, k1, p1, k2.
(11 sts)
Row 6 K3, p5, k3.
Row 7 K2, p1, k2, yo, k1, yo, k2, p1, k2.
(13 sts)
Row 8 K3, p7, k3.
Row 9 K2, p1, k3, yo, k1, yo, k3, p1, k2.
(15 sts)
Row 10 K3, p9, k3.
Row 11 K2, p1, k3, sL1K, k2tog, psso, k3, p1, k2. (13 sts)
Row 12 As row 8.
Row 13 K2, p1, k2, sL1K, k2tog, psso, k2, p1, k2. (11 sts)
Row 14 As row 6.
Row 15 K2, p1, k1, sL1K, k2tog, psso, k1, p1, k2. (9 sts)
Row 16 As row 4.
Row 17 K2, p1, sL1K, k2tog, psso, p1, k2.
(7 sts)

Row 18 As row 2.
Rows 19 to 22 K7.
These 22 rows form patt.
Rep last 22 rows 7 times more, then rows 1 to 18 again, ending with RS facing for next row.

TURN CORNER
Row 1 (RS) K5, turn.
Row 2 K5.
Row 3 K3, turn.
Row 4 K3.
Rows 5 and 6 K7.
Rows 7 to 12 As rows 1 to 6.
Rows 13 to 16 As rows 1 to 4.
These 16 rows complete corner.
Now work patt rows 1 to 22 eleven times, then rows 1 to 18 again, ending with RS facing for next row.
Work corner turning rows 1 to 16 once more.
Now work patt rows 1 to 22 eight times, then rows 1 to 18 again, ending with RS facing for next row.
Work corner turning rows 1 to 16 once more.
Now work patt rows 1 to 22 eleven times, then rows 1 to 18 again, ending with RS facing for next row.
Work corner turning rows 1 to 16 once more.
Bind off.
Join cast-on and bound-off ends of Border.
Sew Border to outer edges of joined Motifs.

Baby slippers

⭐ *Knitted in cool 100 percent cotton, these are the perfect gift for a newborn baby. They will take only an evening or two at most to knit.*

You will need
- 1 x 3¹/₂oz/230yd (100g/210m) ball of a lightweight cotton yarn in lilac
- Pair of size 0 (2mm) knitting needles
- 2 buttons

Gauge and finished size
- 35 stitches and 64 rows to 4in (10cm) over garter stitch using size 0 (2mm) needles.
- Slipper measures 4¹/₂in (11cm) from toe to heel.

Slippers (make 2)
With size 0 (2mm) needles, cast on 22 sts.
Starting with a RS row, work in garter st, inc 1 st at each end of first and foll 7 alt rows. (38 sts)
Work 1 row, ending with RS facing for next row.
Dec 1 st at each end of next and foll 7 alt rows, ending with **WS** facing for next row. (22 sts)
This section forms the sole.
Cast on 8 sts (for heel) at beg of next row. (30 sts)
Inc 1 st at beg of next and foll 7 alt rows, ending with **WS** facing for next row. (38 sts)
Bind off 20 sts (for foot opening) at beg of next row. (18 sts)
Work 19 rows on these 18 sts for top of foot, ending with **WS** facing for next row.
Cast on 20 sts (for other side of foot opening)
at beg of next row. (38 sts)
Dec 1 st at beg of next and foll 7 alt rows, ending with **WS** facing for next row.
Bind off rem 30 sts knitwise (on **WS**).

Finishing
Press following instructions on yarn label. Join straight row-end edges to form heel seam. Easing in fullness of upper section, sew upper section to sole.

Strap
With RS facing and size 0 (2mm) needles, starting 9 sts before heel seam, **pick up and k** 9 sts to heel seam, then 9 sts beyond heel seam. (18 sts)
Working in garter st, cast on 14 sts at beg of next 2 rows. (46 sts)
Work 1 row, ending with RS facing for next row.
LEFT SLIPPER ONLY
Next row K2, bind off 3 sts (to make buttonhole), k to end.
RIGHT SLIPPER ONLY
Next row K to last 5 sts, bind off 3 sts (to make buttonhole), k to end.
BOTH SLIPPERS
Next row K to end, casting on 3 sts over those bound off on previous row.
Work 3 rows, ending with **WS** facing for next row.
Bind off knitwise (on **WS**).
Sew on buttons.

Girl's bolero

⭐ *This ballet-style, wrap-over top is simply a great style to wear, doubling up for ballet practice and for parties.*

You will need
- 4 [**5**, 6, **6**, 7] x 1³⁄₄oz/131yd (50g/120m) balls of a wool-mix, medium-weight yarn in rose pink
- Pair each of size 3 (3¹⁄₄mm) and size 6 (4mm) knitting needles

Gauge and finished size
- 22 stitches and 30 rows to 4in (10cm) over St st using size 6 (4mm) needles.
- To fit approx age 3–4 [**4–5**, 6–7, **8–9**, 10–11] years.
- To fit chest 22 [**24**, 26, **28**, 30]in (56 [**61**, 66, **71**, 76]cm).
- Knitted chest measurement—23 [**25¹⁄₂**, 27¹⁄₂, **29¹⁄₂**, 32¹⁄₂]in (59 [**65**, 70, **75**, 83]cm).
- Finished length—30 [**32**, 36, **39**, 41]cm (12 [**12¹⁄₂**, 14, **15¹⁄₂**, 16]in).
- Sleeve length—9 [**10¹⁄₂**, 12, **14**, 15¹⁄₂]in (23 [**27**, 31, **35**, 39]cm).

Left front
With size 3 (3¹⁄₄mm) needles, cast on 52 [**58**, 64, **70**, 74] sts.
Rib row 1 (RS) *K1, p1; rep from * to last 2 sts, k2.
Rib row 2 *K1, p1; rep from * to end.
These 2 rows form rib.
Cont in rib for 2 [**2**, 2, **2¹⁄₂**, 2¹⁄₂]in (5 [**5**, 5, **6**, 6]cm), ending with **WS** facing for next row.
Next row (WS) Rib 3 [**4**, 4, **5**, 1], *M1 (by picking up horizontal loop lying before next st

and knitting into back of it), rib 9 [**10**, 11, **12**, 8]; rep from * to last 4 [**4**, 5, **5**, 1] sts, M1, rib to end. (58 [**64**, 70, **76**, 84] sts)
Change to size 6 (4mm) needles.
Starting with a k row, work in St st for 4 rows, ending with RS facing for next row.
SHAPE FRONT SLOPE
Dec 1 st at end of next row, and at same edge on foll 6 [**8**, 4, **6**, 8] rows, then on every foll alt row until 37 [**42**, 46, **49**, 56] sts rem.
Work 1 row, ending with RS facing for next row.
SHAPE ARMHOLE
Bind off 2 sts at beg and dec 1 st at end of next row. (34 [**39**, 43, **46**, 53] sts)
Work 1 row.
Dec 1 st at each end of next and every foll alt row until 22 [**25**, 27, **30**, 33] sts rem.
Dec 1 st at front slope edge **only** on 2nd and every foll alt row until 13 [**14**, 15, **17**, 19] sts rem.
Work 5 rows, ending with RS facing for next row.
SHAPE SHOULDER
Bind off 7 [**7**, 8, **9**, 10] sts at beg of next row.
Work 1 row.
Bind off rem 6 [**7**, 7, **8**, 9] sts.

Right front
With size 3 (3¹⁄₄mm) needles, cast on 52 [**58**, 64, **70**, 74] sts.
Rib row 1 (RS) K2, *p1, k1; rep from * to end.
Rib row 2 *P1, k1; rep from * to end.
These 2 rows form rib.
Complete to match Left Front, reversing

shaping and working an extra row before start of armhole and shoulder shaping.

Back

With size 3 (3¼mm) needles, cast on 57 [**63**, 69, **75**, 79] sts.

Rib row 1 (RS), K1, *p1, k1; rep from * to end.

Rib row 2 P1, *k1, p1; rep from * to end.
These 2 rows form rib.

Cont in rib for 2 [**2**, 2, **2½**, 2½]in (5 [**5**, 5, **6**, 6]cm), ending with **WS** facing for next row.

Next row (WS) Rib 4 [**4**, 3, **3**, 1], *M1, rib 7 [**8**, 9, **10**, 7]; rep from * to last 4 [**3**, 3, **2**, 1] sts, M1, rib to end. (65 [**71**, 77, **83**, 91] sts)

Change to size 6 (4mm) needles.

Starting with a k row, work in St st until Back matches Fronts to start of armhole shaping, ending with RS facing for next row.

SHAPE ARMHOLES

Bind off 2 sts at beg of next 2 rows. (61 [**67**, 73, **79**, 87] sts)

Dec 1 st at each end of next and every foll alt row until 49 [**53**, 57, **63**, 67] sts rem.

Cont without shaping until Back matches Fronts to start of shoulder shaping, ending with RS facing for next row.

SHAPE SHOULDERS

Bind off 7 [**7**, 8, **9**, 10] sts at beg of next 2 rows, then 6 [**7**, 7, **8**, 9] sts at beg of foll 2 rows.

Bind off rem 23 [**25**, 27, **29**, 29] sts.

Sleeves

With size 3 (3¼mm) needles, cast on 33 [**35**, 37, **39**, 41] sts.

Work in rib as for Back for 1½ [**2**, 2, **2½**, 2½]in (4 [**5**, 5, **6**, 6]cm), ending with **WS** facing for next row.

Next row (WS) Rib 3 [**3**, 3, **2**, 3], *M1, rib 7 [**5**, 8, **6**, 6]; rep from * to last 2 [**2**, 2, **1**, 2] sts, M1, rib to end. (38 [**42**, 42, **46**, 48] sts)

Change to size 6 (4mm) needles.

Starting with a k row, cont in St st, shaping sides by inc 1 st at each end of 11th [**9th**, 13th, **13th**, 11th] and every foll 12th [**12th**, 14th, **12th**, 12th] row until there are 46 [**52**, 52, **58**, 62] sts.

Cont without shaping until Sleeve meas 9 [**10½**, 12, **14**, 15½]in (23 [**27**, 31, **35**, 39]cm), ending with RS facing for next row.

SHAPE TOP

Bind off 2 sts at beg of next 2 rows. (42 [**48**, 48, **54**, 58] sts)

Dec 1 st at each end of next and every foll alt row to 22 [**22**, 14, **22**, 18] sts, then on every row until 8 sts rem, ending with RS facing for next row.

Bind off rem 8 sts.

Finishing

Press following instructions on yarn label. Join shoulder seams. Join side seams, leaving a 1in (3cm) opening in right side seam above ribbing. Join sleeve seams. Insert Sleeves.

Front borders (both alike)
With size 3 (3¼mm) needles, cast on 9 sts.
Row 1 (RS) K2, (p1, k1) 3 times, k1.
Row 2 (K1, p1) 4 times, k1.
Rep last 2 rows until Border, when slightly
stretched, fits up front opening edge, up front
slope and across to center back neck, sewing
in place as you go along and ending with RS
facing for next row. Bind off.
Join ends of Borders at center back neck.

Ties (make 2)
With size 3 (3¼mm) needles, cast on 9 sts.
Work as for Front Borders until Tie meas
13 [**15**, 15½, **17½**, 19½]in (33 [**38**, 40, **45**,
50]cm), ending with RS facing for next row.
Bind off.
Sew ends of Ties to edges of Front Borders
just above ribbing.
To tie bolero, slip end of left front tie through
opening in right front side seam and tie at
back of bolero.

Child's gloves

⭐⭐⭐ *These cozy gloves are knitted in a lightweight wool-mix yarn, fine enough not to irritate sensitive young skin.*

You will need
- A wool-mix, lightweight yarn, each ball approx 1³/₄oz/201yd (50g/184m):
    - 1 ball in **MC**—purple
    - Small amount of **CC**—green
- Set of four size 2 (2³/₄mm) double-pointed knitting needles

Gauge and finished size
- 32 stitches and 40 rows to 4in (10cm) over St st using size 2 (2³/₄mm) needles.
- Width around hand—5in (13cm).
- Finished length—8¹/₂in (21cm).

Right glove
With size 2 (2³/₄mm) double-pointed needles and CC, cast on 38 sts, distributing sts evenly over 3 needles. (12 sts on first two needles and 14 sts on 3rd needle)
Break off CC and join in MC.
Round 1 (RS) *K1, p1; rep from * to end.
Rep this round 23 times more.
Round 25 (RS) Rib 4, inc in next st, rib 9, inc in next st, rib 8, inc in next st, rib 9, inc in next st, rib 4. (42 sts)
SHAPE FOR THUMB
Rounds 1 to 3 P1, k4, p1, k to end.
Round 4 P1, (inc in next st, k1) twice, p1, k to end. (44 sts)
Rounds 5 to 7 P1, k6, p1, k to end.
Round 8 P1, inc in next st, k3, inc in next st, k1, p1, k to end. (46 sts)

Rounds 9 to 11 P1, k8, p1, k to end.
Round 12 P1, inc in next st, k5, inc in next st, k1, p1, k to end. (48 sts)
Rounds 13 to 15 P1, k10, p1, k to end.
Round 16 P1, inc in next st, k7, inc in next st, k1, p1, k to end. (50 sts)
Rounds 17 to 19 P1, k12, p1, k to end.
Round 20 K1, slip next 12 sts onto a holder for thumb, cast on 2 sts, k to end. (40 sts)
Rounds 21 to 28 Knit.**
SHAPE FIRST FINGER
Next round K6, slip next 29 sts onto a holder, cast on 2 sts, k rem 5 sts. (13 sts)
***Distribute these 13 sts evenly over three needles and cont as foll:
Next round Knit.
Rep last round 23 times more.
Next round (K2tog) 6 times, k1. (7 sts)
Next round K1, (k2tog) 3 times.
Break yarn and thread through rem 4 sts.
Pull up tight and fasten off securely.
SHAPE SECOND FINGER
Next round Rejoin yarn and k first 5 sts from holder, leave next 19 sts on holder, cast on 2 sts, k rem 5 sts on holder, then **pick up and k 2 sts** from base of first finger. (14 sts)
Distribute these 14 sts evenly over three needles and cont as foll:
Next round Knit.
Rep last round 27 times more.
Next round (K2tog) 7 times. (7 sts)
Next round K1, (k2tog) 3 times.
Break yarn and thread through rem 4 sts.
Pull up tight and fasten off securely.***
SHAPE THIRD FINGER
Next round Rejoin yarn and k first 4 sts from

holder, leave next 10 sts on holder, cast on 2 sts, k rem 5 sts on holder, then **pick up and k** 2 sts from base of second finger. (13 sts)
****Distribute these 13 sts evenly over three needles and cont as foll:
Next round Knit.
Rep last round 23 times more.
Next round (K2tog) 6 times, k1. (7 sts)
Next round K1, (k2tog) 3 times.
Break yarn and thread through rem 4 sts.
Pull up tight and fasten off securely.

SHAPE FOURTH FINGER
Next round Rejoin yarn and k 10 sts on holder, then **pick up and k** 2 sts from base of third finger. (12 sts)
Distribute these 12 sts evenly over three needles and cont as foll:
Next round Knit.
Rep last round 16 times more.
Next round (K2tog) 6 times. (6 sts)
Next round (K2tog) 3 times.
Break yarn and thread through rem 3 sts.
Pull up tight and fasten off securely.

SHAPE THUMB
Next round Rejoin yarn and k 12 sts on thumb holder, then **pick up and k** 2 sts from base of hand section. (14 sts)
Distribute these 14 sts evenly over three needles and cont as foll:
Next round Knit.
Rep last round 14 times more.
Next round (K2tog) 7 times. (7 sts)
Next round K1, (k2tog) 3 times.
Break yarn and thread through rem 4 sts.
Pull up tight and fasten off securely.

Left glove
Work as for Right Glove to **.
SHAPE FIRST FINGER
Next round K9, slip next 29 sts onto a holder, cast on 2 sts, k rem 2 sts. (13 sts)
Work as for Right Glove from *** to ***.

SHAPE THIRD FINGER
Next round Rejoin yarn and k first 5 sts from holder, leave next 10 sts on holder, cast on 2 sts, k rem 4 sts on holder, then **pick up and k** 2 sts from base of second finger. (13 sts)
Complete as for Right Glove from ****.

Finishing
Press following instructions on yarn label.

Child's wool cardigan

✪ ✪ *You can make this pattern up for a boy or girl, choosing the colors that you prefer and reversing the button band for a boy.*

You will need
- 5 [**5**, 6, **6**, 6, **7**] x 1³/₄oz/131yd (50g/120m) balls of a wool-mix, medium-weight yarn in desired shade
- Pair each of size 3 (3¹/₄mm) and size 6 (4mm) knitting needles
- 5 [**5**, 6, **6**, 7, **7**] buttons

Gauge and finished size
- 22 stitches and 30 rows to 4in (10cm) over St st using size 6 (4mm) needles.
- To fit approx age 2–3 [**3–4**, 4–5, **6–7**, 8–9, **10–11**] years.
- To fit chest 20 [**22**, 24, **26**, 28, **30**]in (51 [**56**, 61, **66**, 71, **76**]cm).
- Knitted chest measurement—23 [**25**, 27, **29¹/₂**, 31¹/₂, **33¹/₂**]in (58 [**64**, 69, **75**, 80, **85**]cm).
- Finished length—13 [**14**, 16, **18**, 19¹/₂, **21¹/₂**]in (33 [**36**, 41, **46**, 50, **54**]cm).
- Sleeve length—8¹/₂ [**9¹/₂**, 11, **12¹/₂**, 14, **15¹/₂**]in (21 [**24**, 28, **32**, 36, **39**]cm).

Back
With size 3 (3¹/₄mm) needles, cast on 63 [**69**, 75, **81**, 87, **93**] sts.
Rib row 1 (RS) K1, *p1, k1; rep from * to end.
Rib row 2 P1, *k1, p1; rep from * to end.
These 2 rows form rib.
Cont in rib for 1 [**1**, 1¹/₂, **1¹/₂**, 2, **2**]in (2 [**2**, 4, **4**, 5, **5**]cm), inc 1 st at center of last row and ending with RS facing for next row.

(64 [**70**, 76, **82**, 88, **94**] sts)
Change to size 6 (4mm) needles.
Starting with a k row, cont in St st until Back meas 7¹/₂ [**8¹/₂**, 9¹/₂, **11**, 12, **13**]in (19 [**21**, 24, **28**, 31, **33**]cm), ending with RS facing for next row.

SHAPE RAGLAN ARMHOLES
Bind off 2 sts at beg of next 2 rows. (60 [**66**, 72, **78**, 84, **90**] sts)
Next row (RS) K1, sL1K, k1, psso, k to last 3 sts, k2tog, k1.
Next row Purl.
Rep last 2 rows 19 [**21**, 23, **25**, 27, **29**] times more, ending with RS facing for next row.
Bind off rem 20 [**22**, 24, **26**, 28, **30**] sts.

Pocket linings (make 2)
With size 6 (4mm) needles, cast on 15 [**15**, 19, **19**, 23, **23**] sts.
Starting with a k row, work in St st for 3 [**3**, 3, **3**, 3¹/₂, **3¹/₂**]in (7 [**7**, 8, **8**, 9, **9**]cm), ending with RS facing for next row.
Break yarn and leave sts on a holder.

Left front
With size 3 (3¹/₄mm) needles, cast on 31 [**35**, 37, **41**, 43, **47**] sts.
Work in rib as for Back for 1 [**1**, 1¹/₂, **1¹/₂**, 2, **2**]in (2 [**2**, 4, **4**, 5, **5**]cm), inc 1 [**0**, 1, **0**, 1, **0**] st at center of last row and ending with RS facing for next row. (32 [**35**, 38, **41**, 44, **47**] sts)
Change to size 6 (4mm) needles.
Starting with a k row, cont in St st until Left Front meas 3¹/₂ [**3¹/₂**, 4¹/₂, **4¹/₂**, 5¹/₂, **5¹/₂**]in (9 [**9**, 12, **12**, 14, **14**]cm), ending with RS facing for next row.**

PLACE POCKET

Next row (RS) K8 [**9**, 9, **10**, 10, **11**], slip next 15 [**15**, 19, **19**, 23, **23**] sts onto a holder and, in their place, k across 15 [**15**, 19, **19**, 23, **23**] sts of first Pocket Lining, k to end.

Cont without shaping until Left Front matches Back to start of raglan armhole shaping, ending with RS facing for next row.

SHAPE RAGLAN ARMHOLE AND FRONT SLOPE

Next row (RS) Bind off 2 sts, k to last 3 sts, k2tog, k1. (29 [**32**, 35, **38**, 41, **44**] sts)

Working all front slope decreases as set by last row and all raglan armhole decreases as set by Back, dec 1 st at raglan armhole edge of 2nd and every foll alt row **and at same time** dec 1 st at front slope edge on 4th and every foll 4th row until 8 sts rem.

Dec 1 st at raglan armhole edge **only** on 2nd and every foll alt row until 2 sts rem.

Work 1 row, ending with RS facing for next row.

Next row (RS) K2tog and fasten off.

Right front

Work as for Left Front to **.

PLACE POCKET

Next row (RS) K9 [**11**, 10, **12**, 11, **13**], slip next 15 [**15**, 19, **19**, 23, **23**] sts onto a holder and, in their place, k across 15 [**15**, 19, **19**, 23, **23**] sts of second Pocket Lining, k to end. Complete to match Left Front, reversing shaping and working an extra row before start of raglan armhole shaping.

Sleeves

With size 3 (3¼mm) needles, cast on 31 [**33**, 35, **35**, 37, **39**] sts.

Work in rib as for Back for 1 [**1**, 1½, **1½**, 2, **2**]in (2 [**2**, 4, **4**, 5, **5**]cm), inc 3 sts evenly across last row and ending with RS facing for next row. (34 [**36**, 38, **38**, 40, **42**] sts)

Change to size 6 (4mm) needles.

Starting with a k row, cont in St st, shaping sides by inc 1 st at each end of 9th [**9th**, next, **9th**, 3rd, **3rd**] and every foll 10th [**10th**, 10th, **10th**, 11th, **11th**] row until there are 44 [**48**, 52, **52**, 56, **60**] sts.

Cont without shaping until Sleeve meas 8½ [**9½**, 11, **12½**, 14, **15½**]in (21 [**24**, 28, **32**, 36, **39**]cm), ending with RS facing for next row.

SHAPE RAGLAN

Bind off 2 sts at beg of next 2 rows. (40 [**44**, 48, **48**, 52, **56**] sts)

Work 2 rows.

Working all raglan decreases as set by Back, dec 1 st at each end of next and every foll 4th row until 34 [**38**, 42, **38**, 42, **46**] sts rem, then on every foll alt row until 6 sts rem.

Work 1 row, ending with RS facing for next row. Bind off rem 6 sts.

Finishing

Press following instructions on yarn label. Join raglan seams.

Button border

With size 3 (3¼mm) needles, cast on 7 sts.

Row 1 (RS) K2, (p1, k1) twice, k1.

Row 2 (K1, p1) 3 times, k1.

Rep last 2 rows until Border, when slightly stretched, fits up front opening edge (left front for a girl, or right front for a boy), up front slope and across to center back neck, sewing in place as you go along and ending with RS facing for next row. Bind off.

Mark positions for 5 [**5**, 6, **6**, 7, **7**] buttons on this Border—first to come ⅜in (1cm) up from cast-on edge, last to come level with start of front slope shaping, and rem 3 [**3**, 4, **4**, 5, **5**] buttons evenly spaced between.

Buttonhole border

Work to match Button Border, with the addition of 5 [**5**, 6, **6**, 7, **7**] buttonholes worked to correspond with positions marked for buttons.

FOR A GIRL:
To make a buttonhole On a RS row, rib 3, bind off 2 sts, rib to end; then rib back, casting on 2 sts over those bound off on previous row.

FOR A BOY:
To make a buttonhole On a RS row, rib 2, bind off 2 sts, rib to end; then rib back, casting on 2 sts over those bound off on previous row.

FOR BOTH A GIRL AND A BOY:
Join ends of Borders at center back neck.

Pocket tops (both alike)
Slip 15 [**15**, 19, **19**, 23, **23**] sts from pocket holder onto size 3 (3¹⁄₄mm) needles and rejoin yarn with RS facing.
Starting with rib row 1, work in rib as for Back for 4 [**4**, 6, **6**, 8, **8**] rows, ending with RS facing for next row.
Bind off in rib.
Sew Pocket Linings in place on inside, then neatly sew down ends of Pocket Tops. Join side and sleeve seams. Sew on buttons.

Child's cotton sweaters

✪ *These classic sweater patterns, knitted in cotton yarn, are worked here in children's sizes—covering ages three to thirteen. They are great for all-year-round wear. Work the V-neck version or the round-neck version, or make one of each.*

You will need

- A lightweight cotton yarn, each ball approx 3¹/₂oz/230yd (100g/210m):
    - 3 [**3**, 3, **3**, 4, **4**] balls in **MC**—denim blue or blue-green
    - 1 ball in **CC**—light purple or brick red
- Pair each of size 2 (2³/₄mm) and size 3 (3¹/₄mm) knitting needles

Gauge and finished size

- 28 stitches and 36 rows to 4in (10cm) over St st using size 3 (3¹/₄mm) needles.
- To fit approx age 3–4 [**4–5**, 6–7, **8–9**, 10–11, **12–13**] years.
- To fit chest 22 [**24**, 26, **28**, 30, **32**]in (56 [**61**, 66, **71**, 76, **81**]cm).
- Knitted chest measurement—25 [**27**, 29, **31**, 33, **35**]in (64 [**69**, 74, **79**, 84, **89**]cm).
- Finished length—14¹/₂ [**16**, 17¹/₂, **19**, 20, **21¹/₂**]in (37 [**41**, 45, **48**, 51, **54**]cm).
- Sleeve length—10 [**11¹/₂**, 13, **14¹/₂**, 15¹/₂, **16¹/₂**]in (25 [**29**, 33, **37**, 39, **42**]cm).

V-NECK SWEATER

Back

With size 2 (2³/₄mm) needles and CC, cast on 83 [**89**, 97, **103**, 111, **117**] sts.
Break off CC and join in MC.

Beg rib on next row as foll:
Rib row 1 (RS) K1, *p1, k1; rep from * to end.
Rib row 2 P1, *k1, p1; rep from * to end.
These 2 rows form rib.
Cont in rib for 2 [**2**, 2, **2**, 2¹/₂, **2¹/₂**]in (5 [**5**, 5, **5**, 6, **6**]cm), ending with **WS** facing for next row.
Next row (WS) Rib 5 [**5**, 6, 6, 7, 7], * M1 (by picking up horizontal loop lying before next st and knitting into back of it), rib 12 [**13**, 14, **15**, 16, **17**]; rep from * to last 6 [**6**, 7, **7**, 8, **8**] sts, M1, rib to end. (90 [**96**, 104, **110**, 118, **124**] sts)
Change to size 3 (3¹/₄mm) needles.
Starting with a k row, cont in St st until Back meas 8¹/₂ [**9¹/₂**, 10¹/₂, **11¹/₂**, 12, **12¹/₂**]in (21 [**24**, 27, **29**, 30, **32**]cm), ending with RS facing for next row.

SHAPE RAGLAN ARMHOLES
Bind off 2 sts at beg of next 2 rows. (86 [**92**, 100, **106**, 114, **120**] sts)
Next row (RS) K1, sL1K, k1, psso, k to last 3 sts, k2tog, k1. (84 [**90**, 98, **104**, 112, **118**] sts)
Next row Purl.**
Rep last 2 rows 23 [**25**, 28, **30**, 33, **35**] times more, ending with RS facing for next row. (38 [**40**, 42, **44**, 46, **48**] sts)
Next row (RS) K1, sL1K, k2tog, psso, k to last 4 sts, k3tog, k1.
Next row Purl.
Rep last 2 rows twice more.
Break yarn and leave rem 26 [**28**, 30, **32**, 34, **36**] sts on a holder.

Front

Work as for Back to **.

DIVIDE FOR NECK

Next row (RS) K1, sL1K, k1, psso, k36 [**39**, 43, **46**, 50, **53**], k2tog, k1, turn and work this side first.

Working all raglan decreases as set by Back and all neck decreases as set by last row, cont as foll:

Dec 1 st at raglan armhole edge on 2nd and foll 21 [**23**, 26, **28**, 30, **32**] alt rows and **at same time** dec 1 st at neck edge on 4th and every foll 4th row. (7 [**7**, 7, **7**, 8, **8**] sts)

30 and 32in (76 and 81cm) sizes only: Dec 1 st at raglan armhole edge **only** on 2nd row. (7 sts)

All sizes: Working raglan armhole decreases as set by Back, dec 2 sts at raglan armhole edge **only** on 2nd and foll alt row. (3 sts)

Work 1 row, ending with RS facing for next row.

Next row (RS) SL1K, k2tog, psso.

Next row P1 and fasten off.

With RS facing, rejoin yarn to rem sts, k1, sL1K, k1, psso, k to last 3 sts, k2tog, k1. (40 [**43**, 47, **50**, 54, **57**] sts)

Complete to match first side, reversing shaping.

Sleeves

With size 2 (2³/₄mm) needles and CC, cast on 45 [**47**, 49, **51**, 53, **55**] sts.

Break off CC and join in MC.

Work in rib as for Back for 2 [**2**, 2, **2**, 2½, **2½**]in (5 [**5**, 5, **5**, 6, **6**]cm), ending with **WS** facing for next row.

Next row (WS) Rib 7 [**7**, 8, **5**, 4, **5**], * M1, rib 15 [**16**, 16, **10**, 11, **11**]; rep from * to last 8 [**8**, 9, **6**, 5, **6**] sts, M1, rib to end. (48 [**50**, 52, **56**, 58, **60**] sts)

Change to size 3 (3¼mm) needles.

Starting with a k row, cont in St st, shaping sides by inc 1 st at each end of 3rd [**3rd**, 3rd, **7th**, 3rd, **3rd**] and every foll 7th row to 62 [**60**,

68, **68**, 70, **70**] sts, then on every foll 8th row until there are 66 [**70**, 76, **80**, 86, **90**] sts.

Cont without shaping until Sleeve meas 10 [**11½**, 13, **14½**, 15½, **16½**]in (25 [**29**, 33, **37**, 39, **42**]cm), ending with RS facing for next row.

SHAPE RAGLAN

Bind off 2 sts at beg of next 2 rows. (62 [**66**, 72, **76**, 82, **86**] sts)

Working all raglan decreases as set by Back, dec 1 st at each end of next and every foll alt row until 8 sts rem.

Work 1 row, ending with RS facing for next row.

Break yarn and leave rem 8 sts on a holder.

Finishing

Press following instructions on yarn label.

Join both front and right back raglan seams.

Neck border

With RS facing, size 2 (2³/₄mm) needles and MC, k 8 sts from left sleeve, **pick up and k** 44 [**48**, 52, **54**, 60, **62**] sts down left side of neck, 1 st from base of V and mark this st with a colored thread, and 44 [**48**, 52, **54**, 60, **62**] sts up right side of neck, k 8 sts from right sleeve, then 26 [**28**, 30, **32**, 34, **36**] sts from back. (131 [**141**, 151, **157**, 171, **177**] sts)

Row 1 (WS) (P1, k1) to within 2 sts of marked st, p2tog, p marked st, p2tog tbl, (k1, p1) to end.

Row 2 K1, (p1, k1) to within 2 sts of marked st, p2tog, k marked st, p2tog tbl, k1, (p1, k1) to end.

Rep last 2 rows 3 times more, then row 1 again, ending with RS facing for next row.

Break off MC and join in CC.

Using a size 3 (3¼mm) needle and CC, bind off rem 113 [**123**, 133, **139**, 153, **159**] sts in rib, still decreasing either side of marked st as before.

Join left back raglan and Neck Border seam.
Join side and sleeve seams.

ROUND-NECK SWEATER

Back
Work as for Back of V-Neck Sweater (starts
on page 50).

Front
Work as for Back until 46 [**48**, 52, **54**, 58, **60**]
sts rem in raglan armhole shaping.
Work 1 row, ending with RS facing for
next row.

SHAPE NECK
Next row (RS) K1, sL1K, k1, psso, k14 [**14**,
17, **17**, 20, **20**], turn and work this side first.
Working all raglan decreases as set by Back,
cont as foll:
Dec 1 st at neck edge on next 6 [**6**, 8, **8**, 10,
10] rows **and at same time** dec 1 st at raglan
armhole edge on 2nd and every foll alt row.
(7 sts)
Dec 2 sts at raglan armhole edge **only** on
2nd and foll alt row. (3 sts)
Work 1 row, ending with RS facing for
next row.
Next row (RS) SL1K, k2tog, psso.
Next row P1 and fasten off.
With RS facing, slip center 12 [**14**, 12, **14**, 12,
14] sts onto a holder, rejoin yarn to rem sts,
k to last 3 sts, k2tog, k1. (16 [**16**, 19, **19**, 22,
22] sts)
Complete to match first side, reversing
shaping.

Sleeves
Work as for Sleeves of V-Neck Sweater.

Finishing
Press following instructions on yarn label.
Join both front and right back raglan seams.

Neck border
With RS facing, size 2 (2³/₄mm) needles and
MC, k 8 sts from left sleeve, **pick up and k** 12
[**12**, 14, **14**, 16, **16**] sts down left side of neck,
k 12 [**14**, 12, **14**, 12, **14**] sts from front, **pick
up and k** 12 [**12**, 14, **14**, 16, **16**] sts up right
side of neck, k 8 sts from right sleeve, then
26 [**28**, 30, **32**, 34, **36**] sts from back inc 1 st
at center. (79 [**83**, 87, **91**, 95, **99**] sts)
Starting with rib row 2, work in rib as for
Back for 1¹/₂ [**1¹/₂**, 2, **2**, 2¹/₂, **2¹/₂**]in (4 [**4**, 5, **5**,
6, **6**]cm), ending with RS facing for
next row.
Using a size 3 (3¹/₄mm) needle, bind off in rib.
Join left back raglan and Neck Border seam.
Fold Neck Border in half to inside and stitch
in place. Join side and sleeve seams.

Child's raglan sweaters

✪ *Knitted in machine-washable, medium-weight wool yarn, these classic sweaters have raglan sleeves and are very easy to knit. Take your pick of necklines—a round neck or a turtleneck—once the garment pieces are complete.*

You will need
- A wool-mix, medium-weight yarn, each ball approx 1¾oz/131yd (50g/120m): For Round-Neck Sweater, 5 [**5**, 6, **6**, 7] balls in rose pink or light lime—you will need one extra ball for Turtleneck Sweater
- Pair each of size 3 (3¼mm) and size 6 (4mm) knitting needles

Gauge and finished size
- 22 stitches and 30 rows to 4in (10cm) over St st using size 6 (4mm) needles.
- To fit approx age 3–4 [**4–5**, 6–7, **8–9**, 10–11] years.
- To fit chest 22 [**24**, 26, **28**, 30]in (56 [**61**, 66, **71**, 76]cm).
- Knitted chest measurement—23½ [**25½**, 28, **30**, 32½]in (60 [**65**, 71, **76**, 82]cm).
- Finished length—16½ [**17½**, 18, **19½**, 20½]in (42 [**44**, 46, **49**, 52]cm).
- Sleeve length—10½ [**12**, 13½, **15**, 16½]in (27 [**30**, 34, **38**, 42]cm).

Back
With size 3 (3¼mm) needles, cast on 65 [**71**, 77, **83**, 89] sts.
Rib row 1 (RS) K1, *p1, k1; rep from * to end.
Rib row 2 P1, *k1, p1; rep from * to end.

These 2 rows form rib.
Cont in rib for 2 [**2**, 2, **2½**, 2½]in (5 [**5**, 5, **6**, 6]cm), inc 1 st at center of last row and ending with RS facing for next row. (66 [**72**, 78, **84**, 90] sts)
Change to size 6 (4mm) needles.
Starting with a k row, cont in St st until Back meas 10½ [**11**, 11½, **12**, 12½]in (27 [**28**, 29, **30**, 32]cm), ending with RS facing for next row.

SHAPE RAGLAN ARMHOLES
Bind off 1 [**2**, 2, **3**, 4] sts at beg of next 2 rows. (64 [**68**, 74, **78**, 82] sts)
Next row (RS) K1, sL1K, k1, psso, k to last 3 sts, k2tog, k1.
Next row K1, p to last st, k1.
Rep last 2 rows 17 [**19**, 21, **23**, 25] times more, ending with RS facing for next row. (28 [**28**, 30, **30**, 30] sts)

SHAPE BACK NECK
Next row (RS) K1, sL1K, k1, psso, k4, turn and work this side first.
Dec 1 st at neck edge on next 3 rows **and at same time** dec 1 st at raglan armhole edge on 2nd row. (2 sts)
Next row (RS) K2tog.
Next row P1 and fasten off.
With RS facing, slip center 14 [**14**, 16, **16**, 16] sts onto a holder, rejoin yarn to rem sts, k to last 3 sts, k2tog, k1. (6 sts)
Complete to match first side, reversing shaping.

Front
Work as for Back until 32 [**34**, 34, **36**, 38] sts rem in raglan armhole shaping.

Work 1 row, ending with RS facing for next row.

SHAPE FRONT NECK

Next row (RS) K1, sL1K, k1, psso, k8 [**9**, 8, **9**, 10], turn and work this side first.

Dec 1 st at neck edge on next 5 rows **and at same time** dec 1 st at raglan armhole edge on 2nd and foll alt row. (3 [**4**, 3, **4**, 5] sts)

Dec 1 st at raglan armhole edge **only** on next and foll 0 [**1**, 0, **1**, 2] alt rows (2 sts).

Work 1 row, ending with RS facing for next row.

Next row (RS) K2tog.

Next row P1 and fasten off.

With RS facing, slip center 10 [**10**, 12, **12**, 12] sts onto a holder, rejoin yarn to rem sts, k to last 3 sts, k2tog, k1. (10 [**11**, 10, **11**, 12] sts)

Complete to match first side, reversing shaping.

Sleeves

With size 3 (3¼mm) needles, cast on 33 [**33**, 35, **37**, 39] sts.

Work in rib as for Back for 2½in (6cm), ending with **WS** facing for next row.

Next row (WS) Rib 2 [**2**, 3, **2**, 3], *M1, rib 7 [**7**, 7, **8**, 8]; rep from * to last 3 [**3**, 4, **3**, 4] sts, M1, rib to end. (38 [**38**, 40, **42**, 44] sts)

Change to size 6 (4mm) needles.

Starting with a k row, cont in St st, shaping sides by inc 1 st at each end of 5th [**5th**, 7th, **5th**, 3rd] and every foll 8th [**7th**, 7th, **7th**, 7th] row until there are 50 [**56**, 60, **66**, 72] sts.

Cont without shaping until Sleeve meas 10½ [**12**, 13½, **15**, 16½]in (27 [**30**, 34, **38**, 42]cm), ending with RS facing for next row.

SHAPE RAGLAN

Bind off 1 [**2**, 2, **3**, 4] sts at beg of next 2 rows. (48 [**52**, 56, **60**, 64] sts)

Working all raglan decreases as set by Back, dec 1 st at each end of next and every foll alt row until 6 sts rem.

Work 1 row, ending with RS facing for next row.

Break yarn and leave rem 6 sts on a holder.

Finishing

Press following instructions on yarn label.

Join both front and right back raglan seams.

Neck border

With RS facing and size 3 (3¼mm) needles, k 6 sts from left sleeve, **pick up and k** 10 [**11**, 11, **13**, 14] sts down left side of front neck, k 10 [**10**, 12, **12**, 12] sts from front inc 3 sts evenly, **pick up and k** 10 [**11**, 11, **13**, 14] sts up right side of front neck, k 6 sts from right sleeve, **pick up and k** 5 [**6**, 6, **6**, 6] sts down right side of back neck, k 14 [**14**, 16, **16**, 16] sts from back inc 4 sts evenly, then **pick up and k** 5 [**6**, 6, **6**, 6] sts up left side of back neck. (73 [**77**, 81, **85**, 87] sts)

ROUND-NECK SWEATER ONLY:

Starting with rib row 2, work in rib as for Back for 1½ [**2**, 2, **2½**, 3]in (4 [**5**, 5, **6**, 7]cm).

Using a size 6 (4mm) needle, bind off in rib.

Join left back raglan and Neck Border seam. Fold Neck Border in half to inside and stitch in place. Join side and sleeve seams.

TURTLENECK SWEATER ONLY:

Starting with rib row 1, work in rib as for Back for 4 [**4½**, 4½, **4½**, 5½]in (10 [**12**, 12, **12**, 14]cm).

Using a size 6 (4mm) needle, bind off in rib.

Join left back raglan and Neck Border seam, reversing Neck Border seam for last 2 [**2½**, 2½, **2½**, 3]in (5 [**6**, 6, **6**, 7]cm) for turn-back.

Join side and sleeve seams.

Unisex V-neck sweater

✪ *This cool cotton sweater looks good on both sexes. Edging the V-neck, cuffs and ribs in a contrasting color gives it a touch of class.*

You will need

- A lightweight cotton yarn, each ball approx 3¹/₂oz/230yd (100g/210m):
    - 5 [**5**, 5, **5**, 6, **6**] balls in **MC**—brick red
    - 1 ball in **CC**—red
- Pair each of size 2 (2³/₄mm) and size 3 (3¹/₄mm) knitting needles

Gauge and finished size

- 28 stitches and 36 rows to 4in (10cm) over St st using size 3 (3¹/₄mm) needles.
- To fit bust/chest 32 [**34**, 36, **38**, 40, **42**]in (81 [**86**, 91, **97**, 102, **107**]cm).
- Knitted chest measurement—34¹/₂ [**36**, 38¹/₂, **40**, 42¹/₂, **44**]in (88 [**92**, 98, **102**, 108, **112**]cm).
- Finished length—25 [**25¹/₂**, 26¹/₂, **27**, 27, **27¹/₂**]in (64 [**65**, 67, **68**, 69, **70**]cm).
- Sleeve length—17 [**17**, 17¹/₂, **17¹/₂**, 18, **18**]in (43 [**43**, 44, **44**, 46, **46**]cm).

Back

With size 2 (2³/₄mm) needles and CC, cast on 117 [**123**, 131, **137**, 145, **151**] sts.
Break off CC and join in MC.
Rib row 1 (RS) K1, *p1, k1; rep from * to end.
Rib row 2 P1, *k1, p1; rep from * to end.
These 2 rows form rib.
Cont in rib for 2in (5cm), ending with **WS** facing for next row.
Next row (WS) Rib 8 [**9**, 10, **11**, 12, **13**], *M1 (by picking up horizontal loop lying before

next st and knitting into back of it), rib 20 [**21**, 22, **23**, 24, **25**]; rep from * to last 9 [**9**, 11, **11**, 13, **13**] sts, M1, rib to end. (123 [**129**, 137, **143**, 151, **157**] sts)
Change to size 3 (3¹/₄mm) needles.
Starting with a k row, cont in St st until Back meas 16¹/₂in (42cm), ending with RS facing for next row.

SHAPE RAGLAN ARMHOLES
Bind off 2 sts at beg of next 2 rows. (119 [**125**, 133, **139**, 147, **153**] sts)
Next row (RS) K1, k2tog, k to last 3 sts, sL1K, k1, psso, k1.
Working all raglan armhole decreases as set by last row, dec 1 st at each end of 4th [**4th**, 4th, **2nd**, 2nd, **2nd**] and every foll alt row until 43 [**45**, 47, **47**, 53, **55**] sts rem.
Work 1 row, ending with RS facing for next row.
40 and 42in (102 and 107cm) sizes only:
Next row (RS) K1, k2tog, k to last 3 sts, sL1K, k1, psso, k1.
Next row P1, p2tog tbl, p to last 3 sts, p2tog, p1. ([49, **51**] sts)
All sizes:
Break yarn and leave rem 43 [**45**, 47, **47**, 49, **51**] sts on a holder.

Front

Work as for Back until 109 [**115**, 123, **127**, 135, **141**] sts rem in raglan armhole shaping.
Work 1 row, ending with RS facing for next row.
DIVIDE FOR NECK
Next row (RS) K1, k2tog, k51 [**54**, 58, **60**, 64, **67**], turn and work this side first.

Working all raglan armhole decreases as set, dec 1 st at raglan armhole edge on 2nd and every foll alt row **and at same time** dec 1 st at neck edge on next and every foll 3rd row until 7 [**7**, 9, **11**, 12, **13**] sts rem.

Dec 1 st at raglan armhole edge **only** on next [**2nd**, next, **next**, 2nd, **next**] and every foll alt row until 2 [2, 2, **2**, 3, **3**] sts rem, ending with **WS** facing for next row.

32, 34, 36 and 38in (81, 86, 91 and 97cm) sizes only:
Work 1 row.
40 and 42in (102 and 107cm) sizes only:
Next row (WS) P2tog, p1.
All sizes:
Next row K2tog and fasten off.
With RS facing, slip center st onto a holder, rejoin yarn to rem sts, k to last 3 sts, sL1K, k1, psso, k1. (53 [**56**, 60, **62**, 66, **69**] sts)
Complete to match first side, reversing shaping.

Sleeves

With size 2 (2¾mm) needles and CC, cast on 57 [**59**, 61, **61**, 63, **65**] sts.
Break off CC and join in MC.
Work in rib as for Back for 2in (5cm), inc 1 st at center of last row and ending with RS facing for next row. (58 [**60**, 62, **62**, 64, **66**] sts)
Change to size 3 (3¼mm) needles.
Starting with a k row, cont in St st, shaping sides by inc 1 st at each end of 7th [**3rd**, 9th, **5th**, 3rd, **9th**] and every foll 8th [**8th**, 7th, **7th**, 7th, **6th**] row until there are 88 [**92**, 96, **98**, 102, **106**] sts.
Cont without shaping until Sleeve meas 17 [**17**, 17½, **17½**, 18, **18**]in (43 [**43**, 44, **44**, 46, **46**]cm), ending with RS facing for next row.
SHAPE RAGLAN
Bind off 2 sts at beg of next 2 rows. (84 [**88**, 92, **94**, 98, **102**] sts)
Working all raglan armhole decreases as set

by Back, dec 1 st at each end of next and 0 [**0**, 1, **2**, 2, **2**] foll 4th rows, then on every foll alt row until 6 sts rem.
Work 1 row, ending with RS facing for next row.
Break yarn and leave rem 6 sts on a holder.

Finishing

Press following instructions on yarn label.
Join both front and right back raglan seams.

Neck border

With RS facing, size 2 (2¾mm) needles and MC, k 6 sts from left sleeve, **pick up and k** 60 [**66**, 70, **74**, 80, **84**] sts down left side of neck, k st left on holder at base of V and mark this st with a colored thread, **pick up and k** 60 [**66**, 70, **74**, 80, **84**] sts up right side of neck, k 6 sts from right sleeve, then k 43 [**45**, 47, **47**, 49, **51**] sts from back inc 3 sts evenly. (179 [**193**, 203, **211**, 225, **235**] sts)
Row 1 (WS) (P1, k1) to within 2 sts of marked st, p2tog, p marked st, p2tog tbl, (k1, p1) to end.
Row 2 K1, (p1, k1) to within 2 sts of marked st, p2tog, k marked st, p2tog tbl, k1, (p1, k1) to end.
Rep last 2 rows 3 times more, then row 1 again, ending with RS facing for next row.
Break off MC and join in CC.
Using a size 3 (3¼mm) needle, bind off rem 161 [**175**, 185, **193**, 207, **217**] sts in rib, still decreasing either side of marked st as before.
Join left back raglan and Neck Border seam.
Join side and sleeve seams.

Pompom hats

✪✪ *In four sizes, you can make these for all the family. Pick toning colors for the ribbing and the main body of the hat.*

You will need
- A wool-mix, medium-weight yarn, each ball approx 1¾oz/131yd (50g/120m):
  1 [**1**: 2: **2**] balls each in **MC** for hat and in **CC** for ribbing
  1 ball in extra color for contrasting pompom (optional)
- Pair each of size 3 (3¼mm) and size 6 (4mm) knitting needles

Gauge and finished size
- 22 stitches and 30 rows to 4in (10cm) over St st using size 6 (4mm) needles.
- To fit 7–10 years [**11–14 years**, lady, **man**].
- Width around head—18 [**19½**, 21½, **23**]in (46 [**50**, 55, **58**]cm).

To make
With size 3 (3¼mm) needles and CC, cast on 101 [**111**, 121, **127**] sts.
Beg rib on next row as foll:
Rib row 1 (RS) K1, *p1, k1; rep from * to end.
Rib row 2 P1, *k1, p1; rep from * to end.
These 2 rows form rib.
Cont in rib for 4 [**5**, 6, **7**]in (10 [**13**, 15, **18**]cm), ending with RS facing for next row.
Break off CC and join in MC.
Change to size 6 (4mm) needles.
Starting with a k row, work in St st until Hat meas 6 [**7**, 8, **9**]in (15 [**18**, 20, **23**]cm), ending with RS facing for next row.
SHAPE CROWN
Row 1 (RS) K8 [**9**, 10, **13**], k2tog, (k8 [**9**, 10, **10**], k2tog) 8 times, k8 [9, 10, 13], k2tog, k1. (91 [101, 111, 117] sts)
Row 2 and every foll alt row Purl.
Row 3 K7 [**8**, 9, **12**], k2tog, (k7 [**8**, 9, **9**], k2tog) 8 times, k7 [**8**, 9, **12**], k2tog, k1. (81 [**91**, 101, **107**] sts)
Row 5 K6 [**7**, 8, **11**], k2tog, (k6 [**7**, 8, **8**], k2tog) 8 times, k6 [**7**, 8, **11**], k2tog, k1. (71 [**81**, 91, **97**] sts)
Row 7 K5 [**6**, 7, **10**], k2tog, (k5 [**6**, 7, **7**], k2tog) 8 times, k5 [**6**, 7, **10**], k2tog, k1. (61 [**71**, 81, **87**] sts)
Row 9 K4 [**5**, 6, **9**], k2tog, (k4 [**5**, 6, **6**], k2tog)

8 times, k4 [**5**, 6, **9**], k2tog, k1. (51 [**61**, 71, **77**] sts)

Row 11 K3 [**4**, 5, **8**], k2tog, (k3 [**4**, 5, **5**], k2tog) 8 times, k3 [**4**, 5, **8**], k2tog, k1. (41 [**51**, 61, **67**] sts)

Row 13 K2 [**3**, 4, **7**], k2tog, (k2 [**3**, 4, **4**], k2tog) 8 times, k2 [**3**, 4, **7**], k2tog, k1. (31 [**41**, 51, **57**] sts)

Row 15 K1 [**2**, 3, **6**], k2tog, (k1 [**2**, 3, **3**], k2tog) 8 times, k1 [**2**, 3, **6**], k2tog, k1. (21 [**31**, 41, **47**] sts)

11–14 years, lady's and men's sizes only:
Row 17 K[**1**, 2, **5**], k2tog, (k[**1**, 2, **2**], k2tog) 8 times, k[**1**, 2, **5**], k2tog, k1. ([**21**, 31, **37**] sts)

Lady's and men's sizes only:
Row 19 K[1, **4**], k2tog, (k1, k2tog) 8 times, k[1, **4**], k2tog, k1. ([21, **27**] sts)

All sizes:
Next row (WS) Purl.

Next row (K3tog) 0 [**0**, 0, **3**] times, (k2tog) 10 [**10**, 10, **4**] times, (k3tog) 0 [**0**, 0, **3**] times, k1. Break yarn and thread through rem 11 sts. Pull up tight and fasten off securely.

Finishing
Press following instructions on yarn label. Join back seam, reversing seam for first 2 [**2¹/₂**, 3, **3**]in (5 [**6**, 7, **8**]cm) for turn-back. Make a pompom in desired colors. Wind yarn around a piece of cardboard (width of desired pompom) until it is well covered. Slip yarn off cardboard and tie at center. Cut ends and fluff out pompom. Attach to crown of hat.

Cabled sweater

✪✪✪ *This cabled sweater design, with a contrasting stripe around the neck and cuffs, looks good on both men and women. Make it in white with blue accents as here, or choose more funky colors!*

You will need

- A wool-mix, medium-weight yarn, each ball approx 1¾oz/131yd (50g/120m):
  - 11 [**12**, 12] balls in **MC**—off-white
  - 1 ball in **CC**—denim blue
- Pair each of size 3 (3¼mm) and size 6 (4mm) knitting needles
- Cable needle

Gauge and finished size

- 22 stitches and 30 rows to 4in (10cm) over St st using size 6 (4mm) needles.
- Cable panel (26 stitches) measures 3¼in (8.5cm).
- To fit bust/chest 30–32 [**34–36**, 38–40]in (76–81 [**86–91**, 97–102]cm).
- Knitted chest measurement—34½ [**38½**, 43]in (87 [**98**, 109]cm).
- Finished length—24 [**25**, 26]in (61 [**63**, 66]cm).
- Sleeve length—17 [**17½**, 18]in (43 [**45**, 46]cm).

Special abbreviations

C8F = slip next 4 sts onto cable needle and leave at front of work, k4, then k4 from cable needle.
C8B = slip next 4 sts onto cable needle and leave at back of work, k4, then k4 from cable needle.

Back

With size 3 (3¼mm) needles and MC, cast on 103 [**115**, 127] sts.
Beg rib on next row as foll:
**Rib row 1 (RS) K1, *p1, k1; rep from * to end.
Rib row 2 P1, *k1, p1; rep from * to end.
These 2 rows form rib.
Work in rib for 6 rows more, ending with RS facing for next row.
Join in CC.
Row 9 (RS) Using CC, knit.
Using CC and starting with rib row 2, work in rib for 3 rows, ending with RS facing for next row.
Break off CC and cont using MC **only**.
Row 13 (RS) Knit.**
Starting with rib row 2, cont in rib for 7 rows more, ending with RS facing for next row.
Change to size 6 (4mm) needles and **patt** as foll:
Row 1 (RS) K3, (p1, k5) 6 [**7**, 8] times, (p3, k8) twice, p3, (k5, p1) 6 [**7**, 8] times, k3.
Row 2 and every foll alt row P39 [**45**, 51], (k3, p8) twice, k3, p to end.
Rows 3, 5, 7 and 9 As row 1.
Row 11 K3, (p1, k5) 6 [**7**, 8] times, p3, C8F, p3, C8B, p3, (k5, p1) 6 [**7**, 8] times, k3.
Row 12 As row 2.
These 12 rows form patt.
Cont in patt until Back meas 16½in (42cm), ending with RS facing for next row.
SHAPE RAGLAN ARMHOLES
Keeping patt correct, bind off 9 sts at beg of next 2 rows. (85 [**97**, 109] sts)

Next row (RS) K2, sL1K, k2tog, psso, patt to last 5 sts, k3tog, k2. (81 [**93**, 105] sts)
Next row P3, patt to last 3 sts, p3.
Next row K3, patt to last 3 sts, k3.
Next row P3, patt to last 3 sts, p3.
Rep last 4 rows 12 [**14**, 16] times more, then first 2 of these rows again, ending with RS facing for next row.
Bind off rem 29 [**33**, 37] sts.

Front

Work as for Back until 8 rows less have been worked than on Back to start of raglan armhole shaping, ending with RS facing for next row.

DIVIDE FOR NECK

Next row (RS) Patt 51 [**57**, 63] sts, turn and work this side first.
Keeping patt correct, dec 1 st at neck edge on 2nd and foll 4th row. (49 [**55**, 61] sts)
Work 1 row, ending with RS facing for next row.

SHAPE RAGLAN ARMHOLE

Keeping patt correct, bind off 9 sts at beg of next row. (40 [**46**, 52] sts)
Work 1 row.
Working all raglan decreases as set by Back, dec 2 sts at raglan armhole edge of next and every foll 4th row **and at same time** dec 1 st at neck edge on next and every foll 4th row until 7 sts rem.
Dec 2 sts at raglan armhole edge **only** on 4th and foll 4th row. (3 sts)
Work 3 rows, ending with RS facing for next row.
Next row (RS) K3tog.
Next row P1 and fasten off.
With RS facing, slip center st onto a holder, rejoin yarn to rem sts, patt to end. (51 [**57**, 63] sts)
Complete to match first side, reversing shaping.

Sleeves

With size 3 (3¼mm) needles and MC, cast on 45 [**49**, 53] sts.
Work as for Back from ** to **.
Starting with rib row 2, cont in rib for 6 rows more, ending with **WS** facing for next row.
Row 20 (WS) Rib 4 [**2**, 6], *inc in next st, rib 3 [**3**, 2]; rep from * to last 5 [**3**, 8] sts, inc in next st, rib to end. (55 [**61**, 67] sts)
Change to size 6 (4mm) needles and **patt** as foll:
Row 1 (RS) K3 [**0**, 3], (p1, k5) 2 [**3**, 3] times, (p3, k8) twice, p3, (k5, p1) 2 [**3**, 3] times, k3 [**0**, 3].
Row 2 P15 [**18**, 21], (k3, p8) twice, k3, p to end.
Rows 3 to 10 As rows 1 and 2 four times.
Row 11 Inc in first st, k2 [**5**, 2], (p1, k5) 2 [**2**, 3] times, p3, C8F, p3, C8B, p3, (k5, p1) 2 [**2**, 3] times, k2 [**5**, 2], inc in last st. (57 [**63**, 69] sts)
Row 12 P16 [**19**, 22], (k3, p8) twice, k3, p to end.
These 12 rows form patt and start sleeve shaping.
Cont in patt, shaping sides by inc 1 st at each end of 5th and every foll 6th row to 79 [**87**, 95] sts, then on every foll 5th row until there are 87 [**95**, 103] sts, taking inc sts into patt.
Cont without shaping until Sleeve meas 17 [**17½**, 18]in (43 [**45**, 46]cm), ending with RS facing for next row.

SHAPE TOP

Keeping patt correct, bind off 9 sts at beg of next 2 rows. (69 [**77**, 85] sts)
Working all raglan decreases as set by Back, dec 2 sts at each end of next and every foll 4th row until 13 sts rem.
Work 1 row, ending with RS facing for next row.
Bind off rem 13 sts.

Finishing
Press following instructions on yarn label.
Join both front and right back raglan seams.

Neck border
With RS facing, size 3 (3¼mm) needles and
MC, **pick up and k** 13 sts from left sleeve, 64
[**70**, 76] sts down left side of neck, k st left on
holder at base of V and mark this st with a
colored thread, **pick up and k** 64 [**70**, 76] sts
up right side of neck, 13 sts from right
sleeve, then 28 [**32**, 36] sts from back. (183
[**199**, 215] sts)
Row 1 (WS) K1, (p1, k1) to within 2 sts of
marked st, p2tog, p marked st, p2tog tbl, k1,
(p1, k1) to end.
Row 2 (P1, k1) to within 2 sts of marked st,
p2tog, k marked st, p2tog tbl, (k1, p1) to end.
Row 3 As row 1. (177 [**193**, 209] sts)
Join in CC.
Row 4 (RS) Using CC, k to within 2 sts of
marked st, sL1K, k1, psso, k marked st,
k2tog, k to end.
Rows 5 and 6 As rows 1 and 2 but using CC.
Row 7 As row 1 but using CC. (169 [**185**,
201] sts)
Break off CC and cont using MC only.
Row 8 As row 4 but using MC.
Rows 9 and 10 As rows 1 and 2.
Row 11 As row 1.
Using a size 6 (4mm) needle, bind off rem
161 [**177**, 193] sts in rib, still decreasing
either side of marked st as before.
Join left back raglan and Neck Border seam.
Join side and sleeve seams.

Woman's cotton cardigan

✪✪ *This classic slim-fitting cardigan in cotton yarn has a contrasting trim on the neck, cuffs, and pocket tops. Buy buttons to match the chosen contrasting trim for a great effect.*

You will need
- A lightweight cotton yarn, each ball approx 3¹/₂oz/230yd (100g/210m):

    4 [**5**, 5, **5**, 6, **6**] balls in **MC**—purple

    1 ball in **CC**—pink
- Pair each of size 2 (2³/₄mm) and size 3 (3¹/₄mm) knitting needles
- 9 buttons

Gauge and finished size
- 28 stitches and 36 rows to 4in (10cm) over St st using size 3 (3¹/₄mm) needles.
- To fit bust 30 [**32**, 34, **36**, 38, **40**]in (76 [**81**, 86, **91**, 97, **102**]cm).
- Knitted chest measurement—32¹/₂ [**34¹/₂**, 36, **38**, 40¹/₂, **42**]in (83 [**87**, 91, **97**, 103, **107**]cm).
- Finished length—23¹/₂ [**24**, 24¹/₂, **25**, 25¹/₂, **26**]in (60 [**61**, 62, **63**, 65, **66**]cm).
- Sleeve length—16¹/₂ [**16¹/₂**, 17, **17**, 17, **17**]in (42 [**42**, 43, **43**, 43, **43**]cm).

Back
With size 2 (2³/₄mm) needles and CC, cast on 115 [**121**, 127, **135**, 143, **149**] sts.
Break off CC and join in MC.
Rib row 1 (RS) K1, *p1, k1; rep from * to end.
Rib row 2 P1, *k1, p1; rep from * to end.
These 2 rows form rib.
Cont in rib for 2in (5cm), inc 1 st at center of last row and ending with RS facing for next

row. (116 [**122**, 128, **136**, 144, **150**] sts)
Change to size 3 (3¹/₄mm) needles.
Starting with a k row, cont in St st until Back meas 16¹/₂in (42cm), ending with RS facing for next row.

SHAPE ARMHOLES
Bind off 3 sts at beg of next 2 rows. (110 [**116**, 122, **130**, 138, **144**] sts)
Dec 1 st at each end of next 5 [**5**, 5, **7**, 7, **7**] rows, then on foll 10 [**11**, 12, **12**, 14, **15**] alt rows. (80 [**84**, 88, **92**, 96, **100**] sts)
Cont without shaping until armhole meas 7 [**7¹/₂**, 8, **8¹/₂**, 9, **9¹/₂**]in (18 [**19**, 20, **21**, 23, **24**]cm), ending with RS facing for next row.

SHAPE SHOULDERS
Bind off 5 [**5**, 5, **6**, 6, **6**] sts at beg of next 6 [**4**, 2, **8**, 6, **4**] rows, then 6 [**6**, 6, **0**, 7, **7**] sts at beg of foll 2 [**4**, 6, **0**, 2, **4**] rows.
Leave rem 38 [**40**, 42, **44**, 46, **48**] sts on a holder.

Pocket linings (make 2)
With size 3 (3¹/₄mm) needles and MC, cast on 27 [**27**, 27, **31**, 31, **31**] sts.
Starting with a k row, work in St st for 4¹/₂in (11cm), ending with RS facing for next row.
Break yarn and leave sts on a holder.

Left front
With size 2 (2³/₄mm) needles and CC, cast on 57 [**59**, 63, **67**, 71, **73**] sts.
Break off CC and join in MC.
Work in rib as for Back for 2in (5cm), inc 1 st at center of last row and ending with RS facing for next row. (58 [**60**, 64, **68**, 72, **74**] sts)

Change to size 3 (3¼mm) needles.
Starting with a k row, cont in St st until Left Front meas 6½in (16cm), ending with RS facing for next row.**

PLACE POCKET
Next row (RS) K16 [**17**, 19, **19**, 21, **22**], slip next 27 [**27**, 27, **31**, 31, **31**] sts onto a holder and, in their place, k across 27 [**27**, 27, **31**, 31, **31**] sts of first Pocket Lining, k to end. Cont without shaping until Left Front matches Back to start of armhole shaping, ending with RS facing for next row.

SHAPE ARMHOLE
Bind off 3 sts at beg of next row. (55 [**57**, 61, **65**, 69, **71**] sts)
Work 1 row.
Dec 1 st at armhole edge of next 5 [**5**, 5, **7**, 7, **7**] rows, then on foll 10 [**11**, 12, **12**, 14, **15**] alt rows. (40 [**41**, 44, **46**, 48, **49**] sts)
Cont without shaping until 19 [**19**, 21, **21**, 23, **23**] rows less have been worked than on Back to start of shoulder shaping, ending with **WS** facing for next row.

SHAPE NECK
Bind off 9 [**9**, 10, **11**, 12, **13**] sts at beg of next row. (31 [**32**, 34, **35**, 36, **36**] sts)
Dec 1 st at neck edge of next 10 [**10**, 11, **11**, 11, **10**] rows. (21 [**22**, 23, **24**, 25, **26**] sts)
Work 8 [**8**, 9, **9**, 11, **12**] rows, ending with RS facing for next row.

SHAPE SHOULDER
Bind off 5 [**5**, 5, **6**, 6, **6**] sts at beg of next and foll 2 [**1**, 0, **2**, 2, **1**] alt rows, then 0 [**6**, 6, **0**, 0, **7**] sts at beg of foll 0 [**1**, 2, **0**, 0, **1**] alt rows.
Work 1 row.
Bind off rem 6 [**6**, 6, **6**, 7, **7**] sts.

Right Front
Work as for Left Front to **.

PLACE POCKET
Next row (RS) K15 [**16**, 18, **18**, 20, **21**], slip next 27 [**27**, 27, **31**, 31, **31**] sts onto a holder and, in their place, k across 27 [**27**, 27, **31**, 31, **31**] sts of second Pocket Lining, k to end. Complete to match Left Front, reversing shaping and working an extra row before start of armhole, neck, and shoulder shaping.

Sleeves
With size 2 (2¾mm) needles and CC, cast on 53 [**55**, 57, **57**, 59, **61**] sts.
Break off CC and join in MC.
Work in rib as for Back for 2in (5cm), inc 1 st at center of last row and ending with RS facing for next row. (54 [**56**, 58, **58**, 60, **62**] sts)
Change to size 3 (3¼mm) needles.
Starting with a k row, cont in St st, shaping sides by inc 1 st at each end of 11th [**9th**, next, **5th**, 5th, **5th**] and every foll 8th row until there are 82 [**86**, 90, **80**, 76, **72**] sts.
36, 38, and 40in (91, 97, and 102cm) sizes only:
Inc 1 st at each end of every foll 6th row until there are [**92**, 96, **100**] sts.
All sizes:
Cont without shaping until Sleeve meas 16½ [**16½**, 17, **17**, 17, **17**]in (42 [**42**, 43, **43**, 43, **43**]cm), ending with RS facing for next row.
SHAPE TOP
Bind off 3 sts at beg of next 2 rows. (76 [**80**, 84, **86**, 90, **94**] sts)
Dec 1 st at each end of next and foll 20 [**22**, 24, **27**, 29, **31**] alt rows, then on foll 3 [**3**, 3, **1**, 1, **1**] rows, ending with RS facing for next row. Bind off rem 28 sts.

Finishing
Press following instructions on yarn label. Join both shoulder seams.

Neck border
With RS facing, size 2 (2¾mm) needles and MC, starting and ending at front opening

edges, **pick up and k** 22 [**23**, 24, **29**, 30, **31**] sts up right side of neck, k38 [**40**, 42, **44**, 46, **48**] from back inc 1 st at center, then **pick up and k** 22 [**23**, 24, **29**, 30, **31**] sts down left side of neck. (83 [**87**, 91, **103**, 107, **111**] sts) Starting with rib row 2, work in rib as for Back for 10 rows, ending with **WS** facing for next row.
Break off MC and join in CC.
Bind off in rib.

Button border

With size 2 (2³/₄mm) needles and CC, cast on 11 sts.
Break off CC and join in MC.
Row 1 (RS) K2, (p1, k1) 4 times, k1.
Row 2 K1, (p1, k1) 5 times.
Rep these 2 rows until Button Border, when slightly stretched, fits up left front opening edge to top of Neck Border, sewing in place as you go along and ending with **WS** facing for next row.
Break off MC and join in CC.
Bind off in rib.
Mark positions for 9 buttons on this Border— first to come 1cm (³/₈in) up from cast-on edge, last to come in center of Neck Border, and rem 7 buttons evenly spaced between.

Buttonhole border

Work to match Button Border, with the addition of 9 buttonholes worked to correspond with positions marked for buttons.
To make a buttonhole: On a RS row, rib 4, bind off 3 sts, rib to end; then rib back, casting on 3 sts over those bound off on previous row.

Pocket tops (both alike)

Slip 27 [**27**, 27, **31**, 31, **31**] sts from pocket holder onto size 2 (2³/₄mm) needles and

rejoin MC with RS facing.
Starting with rib row 1, work in rib as for Back for ³/₄in (2cm), ending with **WS** facing for next row.
Break off MC and join in CC.
Bind off in rib.
Join side seams. Join sleeve seams. Insert Sleeves. Sew Pocket Linings in place on inside, then neatly sew down ends of Pocket Tops. Sew on buttons.

Boot socks

✪✪ *These classic long gumboot socks are knitted up in really warm Aran yarn, for great insulation on a cold winter's day. They are knitted on four double-pointed needles.*

You will need

- 5 [**5**, 5] x 3½oz/180yd (100g/164m) balls of a wool-mix, Aran-weight yarn in gray or off-white
- Set of four size 6 (4mm) double-pointed knitting needles

Gauge and finished size

- 20 stitches and 26 rows to 4in (10cm) over St st using size 6 (4mm) needles.
- Length of foot—9 [**10**, 11]in (23 [**25**, 28]cm).
- Finished length—15in (38cm).

Sock (make 2)

With size 6 (4mm) double-pointed needles, cast on 52 sts, distributing sts evenly over three needles. (17 sts on first two needles and 18 sts on 3rd needle)
Beg rib as foll:
Round 1 (RS) *K2, p2; rep from * to end.
Rep this round for 4in (10cm), dec 1 st at end of last round. (51 sts—17 sts on each needle)
Cont as foll:
Round 1 (RS) K2tog, k to last 2 sts, k2tog tbl. (49 sts)
Rounds 2 to 6 Knit.
Rounds 7 to 12 As rounds 1 to 6. (47 sts)
Round 13 As round 1. (45 sts)
Round 14 Knit.
Rep last round until work meas 12in (30cm).

SHAPE HEEL

Next round (RS) K11 and turn, slip last 12 sts of previous round onto other end of this needle (23 heel sts now on this needle), and then divide rem 22 instep sts between rem two needles.
Work on 23 heel sts only as foll:
Next row (WS) SL1P, p22, turn.
Next row SL1K, k22, turn.
Rep last 2 rows 9 times more, then first of these rows again, ending with RS facing for next row.
Next row (RS) K13, sL1K, k1, psso, turn.
Next row P4, p2tog, turn.
Next row K5, sL1K, k1, psso, turn.
Next row P6, p2tog, turn.
Cont in this way until all heel sts are on one needle, ending with RS facing for next row.
Next row (RS) K7.
Heel complete.
Slip all 22 sts instep sts onto one needle.
With RS facing and using a spare needle, k rem 6 heel sts, **pick up and k** 15 sts along side of heel, using another needle k 22 instep sts, using another needle **pick up and k** 14 sts along other side of heel, then k other 7 heel sts. (64 sts—21 sts on first needle, 22 instep sts on second needle, and 21 sts on third needle)
Next round (RS) Knit.
Next round K to last 3 sts on first needle, k2tog, k1, k all 22 sts on second needle, work across sts on third needle as foll: k1, k2tog tbl, k to end.
Rep last 2 rounds 9 times more. (44 sts)
Next round (RS) Knit.

Rep last round until work meas 5¹/₂ [**6¹/₂**, 7¹/₂]in (14 [**17**, 19]cm) from knitted-up sts at heel.

Next round (RS) K to last 3 sts on first needle, k2tog, k1, work across sts on second needle as foll: k1, k2tog tbl, k to last 3 sts, k2tog, k1, work across sts on third needle as foll: k1, k2tog tbl, k to end.

Next round Knit.

Rep last 2 rounds 4 times more. (24 sts) Knit across sts on first needle, transferring them onto same needle as last set of sts. Arrange sts so that there are two sets of 12 sts on needles. Fold sock flat so that needles holding sts are next to each other and, using a third needle, bind off sts from both needles together to form toe seam.

Finishing

Press following instructions on yarn label.

Wool gloves

✪✪✪ *You will need to use four double-pointed needles for these gloves, to create a tubular seamless fabric. The yarn chosen is a wool mix, making them really warm for cold winter weather.*

You will need
- A wool-mix, medium-weight yarn, each ball approx 1¾oz/131yd (50g/120m):
    2 [2] balls in **MC**—gray or taupe
    Small amount in **CC**—green or ginger
- Set of four size 3 (3¼mm) double-pointed knitting needles

Gauge and finished size
- 24 stitches and 32 rows to 4in (10cm) over St st using size 3 (3¼mm) needles.
- Width around hand—6½ [8]in (17 [20]cm).
- Finished length—10 [11½]in (25 [29]cm).

Right glove
With size 3 (3¼mm) double-pointed needles and CC, cast on 38 [44] sts, distributing sts evenly over three needles. (12 [15] sts on first two needles and 13 [14] sts on 3rd needle)
Break off CC and join in MC.
Round 1 (RS) *K1, p1; rep from * to end.
Rep this round 21 [23] times more.
Next round (RS) (K11 [13], inc in next st) 3 times, k2. (41 [47] sts)**
SHAPE FOR THUMB
Rounds 1 and 2 K22 [25], p1, k3, p1, k14 [17].
Round 3 K22 [25], p1, inc once in each of next 2 sts, k1, p1, k14 [17]. (43 [49] sts)
Rounds 4 and 5 K22 [25], p1, k5, p1, k14 [17].
Round 6 K22 [25], p1, inc in next st, k2, inc in

next st, k1, p1, k14 [17]. (45 [51] sts)
Rounds 7 and 8 K22 [25], p1, k7, p1, k14 [17].
Round 9 K22 [25], p1, inc in next st, k4, inc in next st, k1, p1, k14 [17]. (47 [53] sts)
Rounds 10 and 11 K22 [25], p1, k9, p1, k14 [17].
Round 12 K22 [25], p1, inc in next st, k6, inc in next st, k1, p1, k14 [17]. (49 [55] sts)
Rounds 13 and 14 K22 [25], p1, k11, p1, k14 [17].
Round 15 K22 [25], p1, inc in next st, k8, inc in next st, k1, p1, k14 [17]. (51 [57] sts)
Rounds 16 and 17 K22 [25], p1, k13, p1, k14 [17].
Larger size only:
Round 18 K25, p1, inc in next st, k10, inc in next st, k1, p1, k17. (59 sts)
Rounds 19 and 20 K25, p1, k15, p1, k17.
Both sizes:
Next round K23 [26], slip next 15 sts onto a holder for thumb, cast on 4 sts, k to end. (40 [48] sts)
Knit 13 [16] rounds.
SHAPE FIRST FINGER
Next round K12 [15] and slip these sts onto a holder, k12 [14], slip rem 16 [19] sts onto a holder, cast on 2 sts. (14 [16] sts)
***Distribute these 14 [16] sts evenly over three needles and cont as foll:
Knit 21 [25] rounds.
Next round (K1, k2tog) 4 [5] times, k2 [1]. (10 [11] sts)
Next round Knit.
Next round (K2tog) 5 times, k0 [1].
Break yarn and thread through rem 5 [6] sts.
Pull up tight and fasten off securely.

SHAPE SECOND FINGER

Next round (RS) Rejoin yarn and k next 5 [**6**] sts after first finger from holder, leave next 18 [**22**] sts on holder, cast on 2 sts, k rem 5 [**6**] sts on holder, then **pick up and k** 2 sts from base of first finger. (14 [**16**] sts) Distribute these 14 [**16**] sts evenly over three needles and cont as foll:
Knit 23 [**27**] rounds.
Next round (K1, k2tog) 4 [**5**] times, k2 [**1**]. (10 [**11**] sts)
Next round Knit.
Next round (K2tog) 5 times, k0 [**1**].
Break yarn and thread through rem 5 [**6**] sts.
Pull up tight and fasten off securely.

SHAPE THIRD FINGER

Next round (RS) Rejoin yarn and k next 5 [**6**] sts after second finger from holder, leave next 8 [**10**] sts on holder, cast on 2 sts, k rem 5 [**6**] sts on holder, then **pick up and k** 2 sts from base of second finger. (14 [**16**] sts) Distribute these 14 [**16**] sts evenly over three needles and cont as foll:
Knit 21 [**25**] rounds.
Next round (K1, k2tog) 4 [**5**] times, k2 [**1**]. (10 [**11**] sts)
Next round Knit.
Next round (K2tog) 5 times, k0 [**1**].
Break yarn and thread through rem 5 [**6**] sts.
Pull up tight and fasten off securely.

SHAPE FOURTH FINGER

Next round Rejoin yarn and k 8 [**10**] sts on holder, then **pick up and k** 2 sts from base of third finger. (10 [**12**] sts) Distribute these 10 [**12**] sts evenly over three needles and cont as foll:
Knit 17 [**21**] rounds.
Next round (K1, k2tog) 3 [**4**] times, k1 [**0**]. (7 [**8**] sts)
Next round Knit.
Next round (K2tog) 3 [**4**] times, k1 [**0**].
Break yarn and thread through rem 4 sts.

Pull up tight and fasten off securely.

SHAPE THUMB

Next round Rejoin yarn and k 15 sts on thumb holder, then **pick up and k** 4 sts from base of hand section. (19 sts) Distribute these 19 sts evenly over three needles and cont as foll:
Knit 20 rounds.
Next round (K1, k2tog) 6 times, k1. (13 sts)
Next round Knit.
Next round K1, (k2tog) 6 times.
Break yarn and thread through rem 7 sts.
Pull up tight and fasten off securely.

Left glove

Work as for Right Glove to **.

SHAPE FOR THUMB

Rounds 1 and 2 K14 [**17**], p1, k3, p1, k22 [**25**].
Round 3 K14 [**17**], p1, inc once in each of next 2 sts, k1, p1, k22 [**25**]. (43 [**49**] sts)
Rounds 4 and 5 K14 [**17**], p1, k5, p1, k22 [**25**].
Round 6 K14 [**17**], p1, inc in next st, k2, inc in next st, k1, p1, k22 [**25**]. (45 [**51**] sts)
Rounds 7 and 8 K14 [**17**], p1, k7, p1, k22 [**25**].
Round 9 K14 [**17**], p1, inc in next st, k4, inc in next st, k1, p1, k22 [**25**]. (47 [**53**] sts)
Rounds 10 and 11 K14 [**17**], p1, k9, p1, k22 [**25**].
Round 12 K14 [**17**], p1, inc in next st, k6, inc in next st, k1, p1, k22 [**25**]. (49 [**55**] sts)
Rounds 13 and 14 K14 [**17**], p1, k11, p1, k22 [**25**].
Round 15 K14 [**17**], p1, inc in next st, k8, inc in next st, k1, p1, k22 [**25**]. (51 [**57**] sts)
Rounds 16 and 17 K14 [**17**], p1, k13, p1, k22 [**25**].
Larger size only:
Round 18 K17, p1, inc in next st, k10, inc in next st, k1, p1, k25. (59 sts)
Rounds 19 and 20 K17, p1, k15, p1, k25.
Both sizes:
Next round K15 [**18**], slip next 15 sts onto a

holder for thumb, cast on 4 sts, k to end.
(40 [**48**] sts)
Knit 13 [**16**] rounds.

SHAPE FIRST FINGER

Next round K19 [**22**] and slip these sts onto a
holder, k12 [**14**], slip rem 9 [**12**] sts onto a
holder, cast on 2 sts. (14 [**16**] sts)
Complete Left Glove as for Right Glove
from ***.

Finishing

Weave in any loose ends.
Press following instructions on yarn label.

Knitting abbreviations

The following are the knitting abbreviations used in this book, plus some extra commonly used ones. Special abbreviations are always given within the pattern.

alt	alternate
approx	approximately
beg	begin(s)(ning)
CC	contrasting color of yarn
cm	centimeter(s)
cn	cable needle
cont	continu(e)(ing)
dec	decreas(e)(ing)
foll	follow(s)(ing)
g	gram(s)
garter st	garter stitch (knit every row)
in	inch(es)
inc	increas(e)(ing); in row instructions, knit (or purl) into front and back of next st to increase one
k	knit
M1	make one stitch by picking up horizontal loop before next stitch and knitting into back of it
M1P	make one stitch by picking up horizontal loop before next stitch and purling into back of it
meas	measure(s)
MC	main color of yarn
mm	millimeters
oz	ounce(s)
p	purl
patt	pattern; or, work in the established pattern stitch
psso	pass slipped stitch over
p2sso	pass 2 slipped stitches over

rem	remain(s)(ing)
rep	repeat(s)(ing)
rev St st	reverse stockinette stitch (purl RS rows, knit WS rows)
RS	right side(s)
sl 1	slip one stitch
sL1K	slip next st knitwise (as if about to knit it) onto right needle without knitting it
sL1P	slip next st purlwise (as if about to purl it) onto right needle without purling it
st(s)	stitch(es)
St st	stockinette stitch (knit RS rows, purl WS rows)
tbl	through back of loop
tog	together
WS	wrong side(s)
yd	yard(s)
yo	yarn over needle

Sizes in patterns
In patterns that have a choice of sizes, the smallest size comes first and the remaining sizes follow inside brackets [ ]. Where there is only one set of figures, it applies to all sizes. Be sure to follow the same size throughout the pattern.

Index

baby slipover 32-34
baby slippers 38-39
binding off 20
blocking 21
boot socks 72-74
buttonbands 22
buttonholes 22

cardigans
    bolero 40-43
    cardigan bands 22
    child's cardigan 46-49
    cotton cardigan 68-71
casting on 10-11
    chain-edge cast-on 12
    with four needles 13
    loop, making a 10
    thumb cast-on 11
Continental knitting 15
crib blanket 35-37
cushion cover 28-29

gauge 9
gloves
    adult's gloves 75-77
    child's gloves 44-45

knit stitch 14, 15, 16

materials and tools 6

neckbands 23
needles 6, 8-9
    circular needle 8
    four needles, working with 6, 8, 13
    holding 14
    sizes 8, 9

pattern abbreviations 78
pattern sizes 78
pompom hats 62-63
pot holder 26-27
pressing garments 21
purl stitch 14, 15, 16, 17

seams
    backstitch 21
    flat 21
    invisible 21
shaping 18-19
socks: boot socks 72-74
stitches
    decreasing 19
    dropped stitches 23
    increasing 18
    knit stitch 14, 15, 16
    picking up 23
    purl stitch 14, 15, 16, 17
    reverse stockinette stitch 17
    stockinette stitch 16
stockinette stitch 16
    reverse stockinette stitch 17
sweaters
    baby slipover 32-34
    cabled sweater 64-67
    child's sweaters 50-57
    raglan sweaters 54-57
    V-neck sweater 23, 58-61

tea cozy 30-31

yarns 6-7
    holding 14, 15
    joining 23
    suppliers 79
    types 7
    weights 7

nd acknowledgments

For stockists and suppliers of yarns, contact your local craft, needlework, or fabric store or contact the companies below.

If you want to find stockists in other countries, contact the main Coats Crafts UK website, below.

Coats and Clark
Consumer services
PO Box 12229
Greenville, South Carolina 29612-0229
(800)648 1479
www.coatsandclark.com

Coats Crafts UK
Lingfield Point
McMullen Road
Darlington
Co. Durham
DL1 1YQ
UK
www.coatscrafts.co.uk

Rowan Yarns Ltd
Westminster Fibers, Inc.
4 Townsend West, Unit 8
Nshua, New Hampshire 03063
(603) 886 5041
(800) 445 9276
www.personalthreads.com/
westminsterfibers.htm

The publishers would like to thank the following people for their help with this book: Hilary Jagger for helping to select the yarn colours and patterns; Sue Whiting for pattern writing and checking; Stella Smith for pattern checking; Elizabeth Tunnicliffe for supplying yarns; Sally Harding for editing and proof-reading; Anne Wilson for the design; John Heseltine for the photography; Kate Simunek for the artwork; and Jayne Emerson and Edward Berry for modeling garments.